KINGSTON PARISH REGISTER
Mathews, Gloucester, and Middlesex Counties, Virginia

Slaves and Slaveholders, 1746–1827

Martha W. McCartney

Genealogical Publishing Company
Baltimore, Maryland

Published by Genealogical Publishing Company
3600 Clipper Mill Rd., #260
Baltimore, MD 21211
Library of Congress Catalogue Card Number 2013954128
ISBN 978-0-8063-1984-1

Made in the United States of America

Front cover photo of Christ Church in Kingston Parish
is reproduced with the kind permission of Ms. Becky Foster Barnhardt.

Contents

Historical Background

Gloucester County, established in 1651, extended from the north side of the York River to the south side of the Piankatank River. Gloucester's easternmost limits were delimited by the Chesapeake Bay, but its westernmost boundary was undefined until King and Queen County was formed in 1691. During the early 1650s Gloucester County was subdivided into four contiguous parishes, civil as well as ecclesiastical districts of the colony's State Church, the Church of England. In 1791 Mathews County was carved out of Gloucester County's northernmost territory. Mathews County's boundaries embraced virtually all of Kingston Parish, formed between 1651 and 1657, but also included some acreage to the south and west, within neighboring Ware Parish. Fortunately for family history researchers, social historians, and students of material culture, substantial portions of Kingston Parish's colonial vestry records and parish register have survived and are in the archives of the Library of Virginia. Collections of Billups family papers, preserved at the College of William and Mary's Swem Library and at the Virginia Historical Society, also contain important information about Kingston Parish's history and parishioners.

The Kingston Parish register documents the dates on which parishioners' births, deaths, baptisms, and marriages occurred, but it also includes the dates on which some of their slaves were born and baptized. No slave marriages were recorded because the enslaved, considered chattel property, lacked civil rights, including the right to legally marry. The parish register's discontinuous dates and pagination and the record books' variable dimensions reveal that three or more volumes were used to document slaves' vital records. Two of these books were in use contemporaneously, presumably because by 1680 Kingston Parish had two churches whose congregations were served by one minister and one vestry.

Although no eyewitness accounts of slave baptisms have come to light, we know that Virginia clergy would have used the rite proscribed by the Church of England and set down in the *Book of Common Prayer*. We also know that a slaveholder typically was called upon to serve as the baptismal candidate's sponsor. By the early eighteenth century the Bishop of London had begun urging the clergy to convert the enslaved to Christianity, sealing their covenant with the rite of baptism. In fact, in 1724 when the Bishop sent a list of queries to the colony's clergy, he asked how successful they had been in Christianizing slaves. Most Virginia clergy admitted that they had made very little headway, citing the language barrier and resistance on the part of slave owners. The Bishop of London was persistent, however, and by the mid-eighteenth century, many Virginia clergy had begun baptizing infant slaves on a regular basis. By that time, growing numbers of the enslaved had become interested in the evangelical or "New Light" religious groups, which promised believers heavenly rewards, including freedom.

Extant portions of the Kingston Parish register reveal that the overwhelming majority of the slaves the clergy baptized were infants who were only a few weeks old. From time to time, adult slaves and young children were baptized, perhaps because they had become interested in adopting their owners' faith or had been converted. Occasionally, a slave's date of death was recorded. Slave baptisms almost always took place on Sunday, traditionally a day the enslaved were given relief from their chores. It was not uncommon for a slaveholder to present two or more slaves for baptism simultaneously. Most of Kingston Parish's slave baptisms were performed during the lengthy ministries of the Rev. John Dixon Jr., who served as rector from December 1750 to March 1770, and that of his successor, the Rev. Thomas Feilde, who served from January 1771 to April 1777. Mr. Feilde baptized several groups of adult slaves during the mid-1770s, men and women who belonged to various owners.

Over the years, the successive clerks of the Kingston Parish vestry, whose spelling skills varied, inscribed the names of slaves and their owners in the parish register. Sometimes, only a slave's date or month of birth was recorded. Birth records were important legal documents because slaves, as personal property, became taxable when they attained a certain age. The compilation of birth records is only one example of the State Church's functioning as a quasigovernmental entity.

Occasionally, slaveholders from the upper part of Ware Parish (for instance, the Pages of Northend plantation and the Claytons of Windsor) had their slaves baptized in Kingston Parish. They probably did so because overland transportation was difficult and Kingston Parish's lower or southerly house-of-worship was more readily accessible than the church in their home parish. At least one man from Christ Church Parish in Middlesex County, on the upper side of the Piankatank River, had his slaves baptized in Kingston Parish, seemingly because he lived closer to Kingston's upper or northerly church, which was located on Queens Creek, a tributary of the Piankatank.

The names borne by most of the slaves listed in the Kingston Parish register were in common use throughout the British colonial world. For instance, the names James, Tom, William, Betty, Hannah, and Sarah appear with great frequency. Tamar, a name the writer of Genesis applied to both sexes, also was very popular in Kingston Parish. Abraham, Esther, Adam and Eve were among the commonly used names of Biblical origin. Kingston Parish's register includes a baby girl named Cleopatra and several named Venus, whereas baby boys called Adonis, Cato, Juno, and Scipio can be found in the register along with numerous males named Caesar. These name choices probably reflect the educated eighteenth century colonist's interest in the classics, just as geographic names like China and Asia suggest an awareness of the wider world. Some infant slaves (Cuffy, Gingo, Linga, and several called Wonnah) bear names that hint at their parents' desire to maintain an overt cultural link to their African ancestry. Several sets of slave twins were baptized in Kingston Parish. Some individuals (mostly males) were identified by their first and last names. The names Frank, Franky, Francis, and Frances were applied to both males and females and there were other unisex names. It is doubtful that many of the slave children, baptized as infants, had an opportunity to participate in Anglican religious practices as they matured, if indeed they cared to do so.

Among the baptized slaves listed in the Kingston Parish register are four people attributed to the parish glebe, the home farm furnished to an incumbent minister. A clergyman's glebe would have comprised an important part of his stipendiary support, particularly in an agrarian economy, and from 1661 on, the colony's assembly began requiring vestries to provide their clergy with a glebe that had a "convenient" house. Most glebes had one or more out-buildings, such as a detached kitchen, barn, or slave quarters, dependencies that usually were situated in relatively close proximity to the main dwelling. A clergyman had the right to occupy his parish's glebe or he could place its buildings and acreage in the hands of tenants, pocketing the income he received. Many Virginia clergy were given use of some slaves and livestock, parish-owned personal property.

Extant vestry records reveal that by 1684, Kingston Parish had begun providing its clergymen with a glebe. The original part of the Kingston Parish glebe, a 433 acre tract claimed and developed by Colonel Richard Dudley in 1665, was located between Pudding (Put-in) and Lendalls (Woodas) Creeks and fronted on the East River. As time went on, that property was expanded. A plat dating to 1712 reveals that the dwelling then associated with the Kingston Parish glebe, whose size had increased to 533 acres, overlooked Put-in Creek, not far from the East River. Kingston Parish's glebe remained intact until 1810, at which time it contained a dwelling on the banks of Woodas Creek, seemingly a replacement for the earlier glebe house.

About This Volume

Around 1920 author, genealogist, and Gloucester County native Sally Nelson Robins (1855–1925) transcribed the names of all of the men, women, and children whose vital records were entered into Kingston Parish's early register books. Working with fragmentary documents that span the years 1746 through 1827, she copied the names of everyone listed in the parish register. More than forty years after Robins completed her handwritten volume, which is preserved in the Virginia Historical Society archives, Emma R. Matheny and Helen K. Yates made their own transcription. It was privately published in 1963 and later was republished by the Clearfield Company, a subsidiary of the Genealogical Publishing Company. Matheny and Yates focused their attention on Kingston Parish's white communicants but failed to include the nearly 1,860 enslaved men, women and children of African descent whose names also appear in the parish register. That deficiency is addressed in this volume.

Information about the enslaved, extracted from the Kingston Parish register and presented in the text that follows, is organized alphabetically. Within that grouping, the names of those listed ascend chronologically. Because phonically-spelled names can be difficult to relate to their modern equivalents, some entries are listed with more than one spelling variation. For example, the register entry for the slave called Seysr can be found by looking at the name "Caesar," where he is listed as "Caesar or Seysr." On the other hand, the register entry for the slave named Tom Pollipus can be found under the name "Tom" but he is also cross-referenced as "Pollipus, Tom." Because there are almost as many phonic variations of slave owners' surnames as there are in slaves' first names, the most commonly used spelling has been provided in this text. For example, Guin and Gwynn appear as Gwyn, Degges as Digges, and Brookes as Brooks.

Occasionally, a parish clerk seems to have entered a slave's name, owner, and date of birth into the register only to repeat the same information a page or so later when recording the date on which the individual was baptized. However, because we cannot rule out the possibility that a slaveholder had two identically named slaves, who were born and baptized on the same dates, both entries have been included. Family history researchers may find recognizable links within slave families, who tended to name children after their kin. One child was identified as a mulatto, the offspring of a white woman and an anonymous male slave. Certain dates given in the register are approximate. For example, one slave purportedly was baptized on February 31st and three others were baptized on June 31st, nonexistent calendar dates.

A list of slaveholders and the years during which they provided information about their slaves is appended to the transcription that follows.

Martha W. McCartney
2013

A

Abby, a slave belonging to Richard Hunley, was baptized on May 13, 1750. Kingston Parish Register, p. 42.

Abby, a slave belonging to [no first name] Robinson, was born in March 1755 and was baptized on April 2, 1755. Kingston Parish Register, p. 81.

Abby, a slave belonging to John Gwyn, was born on May 30, 1757. Kingston Parish Register, p. 48.

Abby, a slave belonging to Captain William Hayes, was born on June 11, 1762. Kingston Parish Register, p. 55.

Abby or Abbe, a slave belonging to Mary Cary, was born in June 1773 and was baptized on July 11, 1773. Kingston Parish Register, p. 75.

Abby, a slave belonging to Thomas Hayes, was born on February 15, 1777, and was baptized on March 23, 1777. Kingston Parish Register, p. 87.

Abby, a slave belonging to Nancy Billups, was born on June 20, 1777, and was baptized on July 27, 1777. Kingston Parish Register, p. 88.

Abigail, a slave belonging to Walter Keeble, was born on December 17, 1758. Kingston Parish Register, p. 50.

Abraham, a slave belonging to the Honorable John Page Esq. of Ware Parish, was baptized on May 5, 1771. Kingston Parish Register, p. 70.

Abraham, a slave belonging to John Gwyn (the son of H. G.), was born on June 19, 1772, and was baptized on July 25, 1773. Kingston Parish Register, p. 71.

Abraham, a slave belonging to William Armistead Esq., was born on June 7, 1773, and was baptized on July 25, 1773. Kingston Parish Register, p. 75.

Abraham, a slave belonging to William White, was born on February 28, 1773, and was baptized on August 1, 1773. Kingston Parish Register, p. 76.

Abraham, a slave belonging to Major John Robinson, was born in April 1774 and was baptized on June 12, 1774. Kingston Parish Register, p. 78.

Abraham, a slave belonging to the Honorable John Page Esq., of Ware Parish, was born in June 1774 and was baptized on August 7, 1774. Kingston Parish Register, p. 78.

Abram, a slave boy belonging to Charles Jones, was born on March 9, 1752. Kingston Parish Register, p. 43.

Abram, a slave belonging to Edward Davis, was born on March 15, 1755. Kingston Parish Register, p. 46.

Abram, a slave belonging to Captain Thomas Smith, was born on June 8, 1760. Kingston Parish Register, p. 52.

Abram, a slave belonging to John Billups, was born on November 1, 1764. Kingston Parish Register, p. 59.

Abram, a slave belong to Thomas Gayle, was born in December 1766. Kingston Parish Register, p. 62.

Abram, a slave belonging to Joseph Billups, was born on January 11, 1767. Kingston Parish Register, p. 63.

Adam, a slave boy belonging to Robert Flippin, was born on November 30, 1752. Kingston Parish Register, p. 43.

Adam, a slave belonging to John Hayes, was born on April 18, 1757. Kingston Parish Register, p. 48.

Adam, a slave belonging to Matthias James, was born in September 1760. Kingston Parish Register, p. 53.

Adam, a slave belonging to George Forrest, was born on November 27, 1761. Kingston Parish Register, p. 54.

Adam, a slave belonging to Isaac Smith, was born in March 1764. Kingston Parish Register, p. 58.

Adam, a slave belonging to Rose Lilly, was born on December 4, 1764. Kingston Parish Register, p. 59.

Adam, a slave belonging to Joel Foster, was born in June 1766. Kingston Parish Register, p. 62.

Adam, a slave belonging to John Hurst, was born on February 17, 1767. Kingston Parish Register, p. 63.

Adam, a slave belonging to Edmund Custis, was born on December 27, 1768. Kingston Parish Register, p. 65.

Adam, a slave belonging to Christopher Gayle, was born in December 1770 and was baptized on March 17, 1771. Kingston Parish Register, p. 67.

Adam, a slave belonging to Thomas Smith, was born on July 14, 1774, and was baptized on August 28, 1774. Kingston Parish Register, p. 78.

Adam, a slave belonging to James Davis, was born on April 11, 1777, and was baptized on June 1, 1777. Kingston Parish Register, p. 88.

Adam, a slave belonging to Henry Hunley, was born on September 14, 1777, and was baptized on October 19, 1777. Kingston Parish Register, p. 89.

Adonis, a slave belonging to William Tabb, was baptized on March 11, 1750. Kingston Parish Register, p. 41.

Agatha, a slave belonging to James Jones, was born on July 29, 1764. Kingston Parish Register, p. 45.

Agathy, a slave belonging to John Tabb, was born in March 1774 and was baptized on April 17, 1774. Kingston Parish Register, p. 77.

Agent, a slave belonging to John Gwyn, was born on July 18, 1752. Kingston Parish Register, p. 43.

Agge, a slave belonging to Elizabeth Green, was born on September 14, 1756. Kingston Parish Register, p. 47.

Agge, a slave belonging to Humphrey Billups, was born on February 13, 1761. Kingston Parish Register, p. 53.

Agge, a slave belonging to Captain William Hayes, was born on June 19, 1763. Kingston Parish Register, p. 57.

Agge, a slave belonging to Matthias James, was born on November 16, 1767. Kingston Parish Register, p. 64.

Agge, a slave belonging to Thomas Poole, was born in September 1772 and was baptized on November 1, 1772. Kingston Parish Register, p. 71.

Agge, an adult slave belonging to Robert Cully, was baptized on September 13, 1772. Kingston Parish Register, p. 72.

Agge, a slave belonging to Captain Thomas Smith, was born in November 1772 and was baptized on January 3, 1773. Kingston Parish Register, p. 74.

Agge, an adult slave belonging to Langley Billups' widow, was baptized on July 4, 1773. Kingston Parish Register, p. 75.

Agge, a slave belonging to Nicholas Westcomb, was born in September 1774 and was baptized on November 13, 1774. Kingston Parish Register, p. 80.

Agge, a slave belonging to Frances Tabb, was born in May 1775 and was baptized on July 9, 1775. Kingston Parish Register, p. 82.

Agge, a slave belonging to William Armistead Esq., was born in September 1775 and was baptized on December 1, 1775. Kingston Parish Register, p. 83.

Agnes, a slave belonging to Mr. Brooks, was baptized on April 29, 1750. Kingston Parish Register, p. 41.

Alice or Alse, a slave belonging to John Read of Middlesex County, was baptized on May 13, 1750. Kingston Parish Register, p. 42.

Alice or Alce, a slave belonging to Major William Plummer, was born in February 1769. Kingston Parish Register, p. 65.

Alice, a slave belonging to George Hunley, was born on September 7, 1769. Kingston Parish Register, p. 66.

Alice, a slave belonging to Robert Cully, was born in July 1773 and was baptized on September 12, 1773. Kingston Parish Register, p. 76.

Alice, a slave belonging to Sir John Peyton, was born in late 1775 or early 1776 and was baptized on March 3, 1776. Kingston Parish Register, p. 84.

Alice, a slave belonging to William Armistead Esq., was born in February 1777 and was baptized on March 16, 1777. Kingston Parish Register, p. 87.

Alice, a slave belonging to John Billups, was born in June 1777 and was baptized on August 10, 1777. Kingston Parish Register, p. 88.

Allen, a slave belonging to Thomas James, was born on September 2, 1805. Kingston Parish Register, p. 90.

Alminia, a slave belonging to Captain George Dudley, was baptized on April 16, 1750. Kingston Parish Register, p. 41.

Ambrose, a slave belonging to Thomas Hayes, was born in August 1758. Kingston Parish Register, p. 50.

America, a slave belonging to Captain George Dudley, was baptized on April 16, 1750. Kingston Parish Register, p. 41.

Amy, a slave belonging to Mrs. Anna Armistead, was born on September 24, 1759. Kingston Parish Register, p. 51.

Amy, a slave belonging to the Honorable John Page of Ware Parish, was born in June 1774 and was baptized on August 7, 1774. Kingston Parish Register, p. 78.

Ann, a slave belonging to William Hayes, was baptized on May 13, 1750. Kingston Parish Register, p. 41.

Ann, a slave belonging to Sarah Forrest, was baptized on May 13, 1750. Kingston Parish Register, p. 42.

Ann, a slave belonging to John Armistead, was baptized on September 30, 1750. Kingston Parish Register, p. 42.

Ann, a slave belonging to Robert Bristow's estate, was born in March 1774 and was baptized on April 10, 1774. Kingston Parish Register, p. 77.

Ann, a slave belonging to Judith Plummer, was born in December 1774 and was baptized on February 5, 1775. Kingston Parish Register, p. 80.

Ann, a slave belonging to Mann Page Esq. of Ware Parish, was born in May 1775 and was baptized on July 9, 1775. Kingston Parish Register, p. 82.

Ann, a slave belonging to William Lilly, was born in July 1775 and was baptized on August 13, 1775. Kingston Parish Register, p. 83.

Anna, a slave belonging to Mrs. Gwyn, was baptized on May 6, 1750. Kingston Parish Register, p. 41.

Anna or Annah, a slave belonging to Frances Lilly, was born on June 28, 1765. Kingston Parish Register, p. 60.

Anna or Annah, a slave belonging to William Callis, was born on January 13, 1769. Kingston Parish Register, p. 65.

Anne, a slave belonging to John Hayes, was baptized on May 27, 1750. Kingston Parish Register, p. 42.

Anthon, a slave belonging to Walter Keeble, was born on March 5, 1759. Kingston Parish Register, p. 50.

Anthony, a slave belonging to Captain George Dudley, was baptized on April 16, 1750. Kingston Parish Register, p. 41.

Anthony or Antony, a slave belonging to William Hodges, was baptized on September 30, 1750. Kingston Parish Register, p. 42.

Anthony, a slave belonging to John Read's estate, was born on June 9, 1760. Kingston Parish Register, p. 52.

Anthony, a slave belonging to John Lilly, was born on November 30, 1760. Kingston Parish Register, p. 53.

Anthony, a slave belonging to John Cary Sr., was born on April 3, 1764. Kingston Parish Register, p. 58.

Anthony, a slave belonging to John Davis, was born on June 14, 1765. Kingston Parish Register, p. 60.

Anthony, a slave belonging to George Alexander Dudley, was born on January 21, 1769. Kingston Parish Register, p. 65.

Anthony, a male slave belonging to Henry Gwyn, was born in March 1771 and was baptized on April 21, 1777. Kingston Parish Register, p. 67.

Anthony, a slave belonging to Henry Gwyn, was baptized on April 21, 1771. Kingston Parish Register, p. 70.

Anthony, a slave belonging to William Hurst, was born on April 19, 1773, and was baptized on May 23, 1773. Kingston Parish Register, p. 74.

Anthony, a slave belonging to Frances Tabb, was born on June 10, 1773, and was baptized on July 25, 1773. Kingston Parish Register, p. 75.

Anthony, a slave belonging to Humphrey Gwyn, was born on July 25, 1773, and was baptized on September 5, 1773. Kingston Parish Register, p. 76.

Anthony, a slave belonging to Joseph Digges, was born on September 28, 1773, and was baptized on November 7, 1773. Kingston Parish Register, p. 76.

Anthony, a slave belonging to Peter Smith, was born in October 1773 and was baptized on December 5, 1773. Kingston Parish Register, p. 76.

Anthony, a slave belonging to Richard Respess, was born in April 1774 and was baptized on June 5, 1774. Kingston Parish Register, p. 78.

Anthony, a slave belonging to John Eddins, was born on February 6, 1776, and was baptized on March 24, 1776. Kingston Parish Register, p. 84.

Anthony Sprig, a 45-year-old slave belonging to Mr. Brooks, was baptized on January 27, 1750. Kingston Parish Register, p. 41.

Armistead, a slave belonging to Edward Hudgins, was born in June 1773 and was baptized on July 11, 1773. Kingston Parish Register, p. 75.

Armistead, a slave belonging to Thomas James, was born on April 10, 1810. Kingston Parish Register, p. 90.

Arriana, a slave belonging to William Armistead Esq., was born in October 1773 and was baptized on November 28, 1773. Kingston Parish Register, p. 76.

Asia, a slave belonging to Mrs. Anna Armistead, was born on July 26, 1757. Kingston Parish Register, p. 48.

Avisa, a slave belonging to John King, was born in August 1774 and was baptized on September 18, 1774. Kingston Parish Register, p. 79.

Avy, a slave belonging to Matthew Whiting, was born on August 7, 1768. Kingston Parish Register, p. 65.

B

Bama, a slave belonging to Ann Turner, was born on May 20, 1766. Kingston Parish Register, p. 62.

Barber, Jack. See Jack Barber.

Barnabas, a slave belonging to John Gwyn, was born on September 9, 1751. Kingston Parish Register, p. 43.

Barnaby, a slave belonging to Mr. Blacknall, was baptized on April 16, 1750. Kingston Parish Register, p. 41.

Barnaby, a slave belonging to Joel Foster, was born in February 1777 and was baptized on April 6, 1777. Kingston Parish Register, p. 87.

Barney, a slave belonging to John Gwyn, was born on August 5, 1757. Kingston Parish Register, p. 48.

Barney or Barny, a slave belonging to Benjamin Read, was born in February 1768. Kingston Parish Register, p. 64.

Barney or Barny, a slave belonging to Robert Cully, was born in May 1771 and was baptized on June 9, 1771. Kingston Parish Register, p. 68.

Barney or Barny, a slave belonging to Humphrey Gwyn, was born in May 1775 and was baptized on June 16, 1775. Kingston Parish Register, p. 82.

Barney or Barny, a slave belonging to Humphrey Gwyn, was born in June 1775 and was baptized on July 16, 1775. Kingston Parish Register, p. 82.

Beck, a slave belonging to Madam Smith, was baptized on April 29, 1750. Kingston Parish Register, p. 41.

Beck, a slave belonging to John Foster, was born on May 28, 1750. Kingston Parish Register, p. 44.

Beck, a slave girl belonging to Robert Smith, was born on December 26, 1752. Kingston Parish Register, p. 43.

Beck, a slave belonging to William Hayes, was born on September 4, 1755. Kingston Parish Register, p. 46.

Beck, a slave belonging to Moses Hudgins, was born in August 1756. Kingston Parish Register, p. 47.

Beck, a slave belonging to William Hayes, was born in February 1760. Kingston Parish Register, p. 52.

Beck, a slave belonging to Kemp Whiting, was born in March 1761. Kingston Parish Register, p. 54.

Beck, a slave belonging to William Hudgins, was born on July 8, 1761. Kingston Parish Register, p. 54.

Beck, a slave belonging to John Eddins, was born on December 7, 1761. Kingston Parish Register, p. 55.

Beck, a slave belonging to John Hayes, was born on September 24, 1764. Kingston Parish Register, p. 59.

Beck, a slave belonging to Robert Cully, was born on August 7, 1768. Kingston Parish Register, p. 65.

Beck, a slave belonging to Isaac Smith, was born on October 5, 1768. Kingston Parish Register, p. 65.

Beck, a slave belonging to Robert Cully, was born in February 1770. Kingston Parish Register, p. 66.

Beck, an adult slave belonging to John Machen, was baptized on August 30, 1772. Kingston Parish Register, p. 72.

Beck, a slave belonging to William Lilly, was born in February 1773 and was baptized on May 9, 1773. Kingston Parish Register, p. 73.

Beck, a slave belonging to John Hayes, was born in March 1774 and was baptized on April 10, 1774. Kingston Parish Register, p. 77.

Beck, a slave belonging to Robert Bristow's estate, was born on April 13, 1775, and was baptized on May 7, 1775. Kingston Parish Register, p. 81.

Beck, a slave belonging to Matthias James, was born in March 1776 and was baptized on June 16, 1776. Kingston Parish Register, p. 85.

Beck, a slave belonging to Mrs. Lux, was born in July 1776 and was baptized on September 8, 1776. Kingston Parish Register, p. 86.

Beckah, a slave belonging to Capt. Francis Armistead, was born on April 20, 1772, and was baptized on June 21, 1772. Kingston Parish Register, p. 69.

Ben, a slave belonging to Hugh Gwyn, was baptized on April 29, 1750. Kingston Parish Register, p. 41.

Ben, a slave boy belonging to John Gwyn, was born on December 30, 1752. Kingston Parish Register, p. 43.

Ben, a slave belonging to John Gwyn, died on December 22, 1753. Kingston Parish Register, p. 179.

Ben, a slave belonging to John Gwyn, was born on July 8, 1758. Kingston Parish Register, p. 50.

Ben, a slave belonging to Robert Billups, was born on July 23, 1761. Kingston Parish Register, p. 54.

Ben, a slave belonging to William White, was born in October 1767. Kingston Parish Register, p. 64.

Ben, a slave belonging to John Armistead, was born on October 6, 1767. Kingston Parish Register, p. 64.

Ben, a slave belonging to William Callis, was born on May 1, 1768. Kingston Parish Register, p. 64.

Ben, a slave belonging to Major William Plummer, was born in December 1768. Kingston Parish Register, p. 65.

Ben, a slave belonging to William White, was born in October 1770. Kingston Parish Register, p. 66.

Ben, a slave belonging to William White, was born on October 15, 1770, and was baptized on January 20, 1771. Kingston Parish Register, p. 67.

Ben, a slave belonging to Isaac Smith, was born on April 11, 1773, and was baptized on May 9, 1773. Kingston Parish Register, p. 74.

Ben, a slave belonging to Robert Spencer, was born in November 1772 and was baptized on January 3, 1773. Kingston Parish Register, p. 74.

Ben, a slave belonging to Gabriel Miller, was born on February 16, 1776, and was baptized on March 24, 1776. Kingston Parish Register, p. 84.

Ben, a slave belonging to Edward Davis, was born on March 10, 1778. Kingston Parish Register, p. 89.

Ben Wilson, a slave belonging to Rose Lilly, was born in November 1770, and was baptized on March 3, 1771. Kingston Parish Register, p. 67.

Benjamin, a slave belonging to Letitia Ransone, was baptized on September 16, 1750. Kingston Parish Register, p. 42.

Benjamin Tabb, a 30-year-old slave belonging to William Tabb, was baptized on January 27, 1750. Kingston Parish Register, p. 41.

Bess, a slave belonging to Robert Bristow, was born in August 1777 and was baptized on November 23, 1777. Kingston Parish Register, p. 89.

Bet, an adult slave belonging to Widow Hudgins, was baptized on December 26, 1774. Kingston Parish Register, p. 80.

Betsy, a slave belonging to Richard Matthews, was born in March 1773 and was baptized on June 20, 1773. Kingston Parish Register, p. 74.

Betsy, a slave belonging to William Armistead, was born on October 30, 1774, and was baptized on December 18, 1775. Kingston Parish Register, p. 80.

Betsy, a slave belonging to Mann Page Esq. of Ware Parish, was born in August 1775 and was baptized on October 15, 1775. Kingston Parish Register, p. 83.

Betty, a slave belonging to Mrs. Armistead, was baptized on April 29, 1750. Kingston Parish Register, p. 41.

Betty, a slave belonging to John Read of Middlesex County, was baptized on May 13, 1750. Kingston Parish Register, p. 42.

Betty, a slave belonging to Letitia Ransone, was baptized on September 16, 1750. Kingston Parish Register, p. 42.

Betty, a slave belonging to Mrs. Ann Blacknall, was born on January 15, 1755. Kingston Parish Register, p. 46.

Betty, a slave belonging to Joseph Gayle, was born in November 1756. Kingston Parish Register, p. 47.

Betty, a slave belonging to John Read's estate, was born in May 1757. Kingston Parish Register, p. 48.

Betty, a slave belonging to John Davis, the sheriff, was born on December 25, 1759. Kingston Parish Register, p. 51.

Betty, a slave belonging to Sarah Hunley, was born on April 14, 1764. Kingston Parish Register, p. 58.

Betty, a slave belonging to William Tompkins, was born on December 31, 1764. Kingston Parish Register, p. 59.

Betty, a slave belonging to Capt. Thomas Boswell of Ware Parish, was born on May 17, 1766. Kingston Parish Register, p. 62.

Betty, a slave belonging to John Hewel or Huel, was born in June 1767. Kingston Parish Register, p. 63.

Betty, a slave belonging to Capt. Robert Billups, was born on January 20, 1775. Kingston Parish Register, p. 65.

Betty, a slave belonging to John Callis, was born on January 30, 1769. Kingston Parish Register, p. 65.

Betty, a slave belonging to Catherine Spencer, was born on April 17, 1770. Kingston Parish Register, p. 66.

Betty, a slave belonging to George Brooks, was born on April 17, 1772, and was baptized on June 21, 1772. Kingston Parish Register, p. 69.

Betty, an adult slave belonging to Francis Tabb, was baptized on August 30, 1772. Kingston Parish Register, p. 72.

Betty, an adult slave belonging to [no first name] Brooks, was baptized on August 30, 1772. Kingston Parish Register, p. 72.

Betty, a slave belonging to Letitia Ransone, was born on September 11, 1772, and was baptized on October 11, 1772. Kingston Parish Register, p. 71.

Betty, an adult slave belonging to John Almon, was baptized on September 13, 1772. Kingston Parish Register, p. 73.

Betty, a slave belonging to Capt. Thomas Smith, was born in March 1773 and was baptized on February 27, 1774. Kingston Parish Register, p. 77.

Betty, a slave belonging to Capt. Robert Billups, was born on January 2, 1775, and was baptized on February 26, 1775. Kingston Parish Register, p. 80.

Betty, a slave belonging to Samuel Williams, was born on April 14, 1776, and was baptized on June 30, 1776. Kingston Parish Register, p. 85.

Betty, a slave belonging to Thomas Poole, was born in September or October 1776 and was baptized on December 29, 1776. Kingston Parish Register, p. 86.

Betty, a slave belonging to Henry Knight, was born on August 31, 1777, and was baptized on October 5, 1777. Kingston Parish Register, p. 88.

Betty Jones, a small slave girl belonging to William Merchant, was born in April 1777 and was baptized on October 5, 1777. Kingston Parish Register, p. 88.

Beverley, a slave belonging to Thomas Iverson, was born in March 1775 and was baptized on April 30, 1775. Kingston Parish Register, p. 81.

Billy, a slave belonging to Capt. George Dudley, was baptized on April 16, 1750. Kingston Parish Register, p. 41.

Billy, a slave belonging to John Cary Jr., was born on June 4, 1762. Kingston Parish Register, p. 55.

Billy, a slave belonging to Bristow's estate, was born in May 1770. Kingston Parish Register, p. 66.

Billy, a slave belonging to Henry Whiting, was born in October 1770. Kingston Parish Register, p. 66.

Billy, a slave belonging to Henry Whiting, was born in October 1770 and was baptized on January 20, 1771. Kingston Parish Register, p. 67.

Billy, a slave belonging to Franky Tabb, was born in September 1772 and was baptized on November 1, 1772. Kingston Parish Register, p. 71.

Billy, a slave belonging to the Honorable John Page Esq. of Ware Parish, was born in February 1773 and was baptized on May 2, 1773. Kingston Parish Register, p. 74.

Billy, a slave belonging to Mary Plummer, was born on March 9, 1776, and was baptized on May 5, 1776. Kingston Parish Register, p. 84.

Blender, a slave belonging to James Purcell, was born in March 1767. Kingston Parish Register, p. 63.

Bob, a slave belonging to George Keeble, was born on August 15, 1754. Kingston Parish Register, p. 45.

Bob, a slave belonging to John Newell, was born in July 1758. Kingston Parish Register, p. 50.

Bob, a slave belonging to Ann Hunley, was born on June 5, 1759. Kingston Parish Register, p. 51.

Bob, a slave belonging to Anna Armistead, was born on August 5, 1759. Kingston Parish Register, p. 51.

Bob, a slave belonging to Francis Armistead, was born on August 29, 1759. Kingston Parish Register, p. 51.

~~Bob, a slave belonging to Anthony Singleton, was born on June 28, 1763.~~ Kingston Parish Register, p. 57. *Note: this register entry was crossed out.*

Bob, a slave belonging to Gabriel Miller, was born on September 29, 1764. Kingston Parish Register, p. 59.

Bob, a slave belonging to William Lilly, was born in August 1769. Kingston Parish Register, p. 66.

Bob, a slave belonging to Robert Matthews, was born on October 5, 1771, and was baptized on November 10, 1771. Kingston Parish Register, p. 68.

Bob and Harry, twin slaves belonging to John Eddins Jr., were born on June 21, 1772, and were baptized on July 5, 1772. Kingston Parish Register, p. 69.

Bob, a slave belonging to Sir John Peyton, was born in February 1773 and was baptized on April 4, 1773. Kingston Parish Register, p. 73.

Bob, an adult slave belonging to [no first name] Digges, was baptized on July 4, 1773. Kingston Parish Register, p. 75.

Bob, a slave belonging to Sterling Thornton, was born in April 1774 and was baptized on July 10, 1774. Kingston Parish Register, p. 78.

Bob, a slave belonging to Charles Jones' estate, was born in March 1775 and was baptized on May 7, 1775. Kingston Parish Register, p. 81.

Bob, a slave belonging to John Wiley, was born in April 1777 and was baptized on June 1, 1777. Kingston Parish Register, p. 88.

Bob, a 10-year-old slave belonging to James Harris, was baptized on July 2, 1775. Kingston Parish Register, p. 82.

Boston, an adult slave belonging to Christopher Brown, was baptized in 1772. Kingston Parish Register, p. 69.

Bradlam, a slave belonging to William Tompkins, was born on June 12, 1767. Kingston Parish Register, p. 63.

Bristol, an adult slave belonging to William Lilly, was baptized on August 30, 1772. Kingston Parish Register, p. 72.

Brown, Thomas. See Thomas Brown.

Buck, an adult slave belonging to Jasper Clayton of Ware Parish, was born in April 1777 and was baptized on June 15, 1777. Kingston Parish Register, p. 88.

Buck, John. See John Buck.

C

Caesar or Seyser, a slave boy belonging to Gwyn Read, was born on January 15, 1749. Kingston Parish Register, p. 103.

Caesar or Sesr, a slave belonging to Mr. Debman, was baptized on March 11, 1750. Kingston Parish Register, p. 41.

Caesar or Cesar, a slave belonging to Major Dudley, was baptized on April 29, 1750. Kingston Parish Register, p. 41.

Caesar or Cesar, a slave boy belonging to Harry Gwyn, was born on May 29, 1752. Kingston Parish Register, p. 43.

Caesar or Ceasar, a slave belonging to Thomas Smith, was born in May 1758. Kingston Parish Register, p. 49.

Caesar or Cesar, a slave belonging to Major Kemp Plummer, was born in November 1760. Kingston Parish Register, p. 51.

Caesar or Ceasar, a slave belonging to William Hayes, was born on February 19, 1761. Kingston Parish Register, 53.

Caesar or Ceasar, a slave belonging to Matthew Whiting, was born on December 18, 1762. Kingston Parish Register 56.

Caesar or Ceasar, a slave belonging to John Lilly, was born on October 12, 1764. Kingston Parish Register, p. 59.

Caesar or Ceasar, a slave belonging to Edward Davis, was born on May 2, 1766. Kingston Parish Register, p. 62.

Caesar or Ceasar, a slave belonging to Capt. Gwyn Read's estate, was born in July 1766. Kingston Parish Register, p. 62.

Caesar or Ceasar, a slave belonging to John Davis, was born on February 5, 1767. Kingston Parish Register, p. 63.

Caesar or Ceasar, an adult slave belonging to Joseph Digges, was baptized on September 13, 1772. Kingston Parish Register, p. 72.

Caesar, a slave belonging to John Willis, was born in February 1773 and was baptized on February 28, 1773. Kingston Parish Register, p. 73.

Caesar, a slave belonging to Major William Plummer, was born in April 1773, and was baptized on July 4, 1773. Kingston Parish Register, p. 74.

Caesar, a slave belonging to Robert Cully, was born in July 1773 and was baptized on September 12, 1773. Kingston Parish Register, p. 76.

Caesar, a slave belonging to John Elliott Sr., was born on April 13, 1774, and was baptized on May 15, 1774. Kingston Parish Register, p. 78.

Caesar, a slave child belonging to John Foster, was born in July 1775 and was baptized on July 16, 1775. Kingston Parish Register, p. 83.

Caesar, a slave belonging to John Foster, was baptized on July 16, 1775. Kingston Parish Register, p. 82.

Cain, a slave belonging to John Tabb, was born in September 1772 and was baptized on November 1, 1772. Kingston Parish Register, p. 71.

Cain and Mahala, twin slaves belonging to Thomas James, were born on January 8, 1826. Kingston Parish Register, p. 90.

Caroline, a slave belonging to Sir John Peyton, was baptized on June 31, 1772. Kingston Parish Register, p. 70.

Cate, a slave belonging to James Ransone, was born on January 12, 1756. Kingston Parish Register, p. 47.

Cate, a slave belonging to John Hayes, was born in April 1758. Kingston Parish Register, p. 49.

Cate, a slave belonging to Ralph Armistead, was born on July 10, 1759. Kingston Parish Register, p. 51.

Cate, a slave belonging to John Davis Sr., was born on March 7, 1761. Kingston Parish Register, p. 54.

Cate, a slave belonging to Capt. Thomas Smith, was born on May 30, 1761. Kingston Parish Register, p. 54.

Cate, a slave belonging to Josiah Foster, was born on July 18, 1762. Kingston Parish Register, p. 55.

Cate, a slave belonging to James Davis, was born in March 1764. Kingston Parish Register, p. 58.

Cate, a slave belonging to John Cary Jr., was born on April 6, 1765. Kingston Parish Register, p. 60.

Cate, a slave belonging to Humphrey Billups, was born in July 1769. Kingston Parish Register, p. 66.

Catherine, a slave belonging to Samuel Williams, was born in June 1775 and was baptized on July 2, 1775. Kingston Parish Register, p. 81.

Catinoe, a slave girl belonging to Ann Armistead, was born on February 19, 1752. Kingston Parish Register, p. 43.

Cato, a slave belonging to Elizabeth Jones, was born in April 1774 and was baptized on June 12, 1774. Kingston Parish Register, p. 78.

Cato, a slave belonging to Richard Respess, was born in March 1775 and was baptized on July 30, 1775. Kingston Parish Register, p. 83.

Cato or Catto, a slave belonging to Mrs. Mary Cunningham, was born on October 9, 1747. Kingston Parish Register, p. 103.

Caty, a slave belonging to Margaret Wyatt, was born in February 1773 and was baptized on April 4, 1773. Kingston Parish Register, p. 73.

Caty, a slave belonging to Tinsley or Tindsley Dixon, was born in December 1772 and was baptized on May 9, 1773. Kingston Parish Register, p. 73.

Caty, a slave belonging to Sir John Peyton, was born in February 1773 and was baptized on May 16, 1773. Kingston Parish Register, p. 74.

Caty, a slave belonging to John Eddins, was born on March 11, 1774, and was baptized on May 8, 1774. Kingston Parish Register, p. 77.

Caty, a slave belonging to George Brooks, was born in August 1774 and was baptized on November 6, 1774. Kingston Parish Register, p. 79.

Celia, a slave belonging to Mrs. Mary Dudley, was born in July 1759. Kingston Parish Register, p. 51.

Chainy, a slave belonging to Capt. William Hayes, was born on June 17, 1762. Kingston Parish Register, p. 55.

Chainy, a slave belonging to Joseph Billups, was born on April 14, 1765. Kingston Parish Register, p. 60.

Charity, a slave belonging to Thomas Billups, was born on July 1, 1770. Kingston Parish Register, p. 66.

Charles, a slave belonging to William Elliott, was baptized on March 11, 1750. Kingston Parish Register, p. 41.

Charles, a slave belonging to Capt. George Dudley, was baptized on April 16, 1750. Kingston Parish Register, p. 41.

Charles, a slave belonging to William Hayes, was born on June 13, 1758. Kingston Parish Register, p. 49.

Charles, a slave belonging to John Cary Jr., was born on June 4, 1762. Kingston Parish Register, p. 55.

Charles, a slave belonging to John Eddins, was born on December 6, 1763. Kingston Parish Register, p. 58.

Charles, a slave belonging to Elizabeth Lux, was born on August 30, 1765. Kingston Parish Register, p. 60.

Charles, a slave belonging to William Armistead Esq., was born on November 4, 1770. Kingston Parish Register, p. 66.

Charles, a slave belonging to Joseph King, was born in July 1773 and was baptized on September 5, 1773. Kingston Parish Register, p. 76.

Charles and Sarah, adult slaves belonging to William Merchant, were born in April 1777 and were baptized on June 15, 1777. Kingston Parish Register, p. 88.

Charles, a slave belonging to Harry Gwyn, was born on August 17, 1777, and was baptized on October 19, 1777. Kingston Parish Register, p. 89.

Charlotte or Charlote, a slave belonging to Capt. George Dudley, was baptized on April 16, 1750. Kingston Parish Register, p. 41.

China, a slave belonging to Thomas Hayes Jr., was born in January 1760. Kingston Parish Register, p. 52.

China, a slave belonging to John Billups, was born in October 1765. Kingston Parish Register, p. 61.

China, a slave belonging to Banister Harper, was born on February 27, 1772, and was baptized on July 5, 1772. Kingston Parish Register, p. 69.

China, a slave belonging to Mrs. Tabb, was born in July 1772 and was baptized on August 23, 1772. Kingston Parish Register, p. 71.

China, a slave belonging to Humphrey Gwyn, was born in February 1773 and was baptized on May 9, 1773. Kingston Parish Register, p. 73.

China, a slave belonging to Anna Billups, was born on March 18, 1774, and was baptized on May 8, 1774. Kingston Parish Register, p. 77.

China, a slave belonging to William Plummer's estate, was born on July 30, 1774, and was baptized on September 25, 1774. Kingston Parish Register, p. 79.

China, a slave belonging to Major Thomas Smith, was born on August 7, 1774, and was baptized on September 11, 1774. Kingston Parish Register, p. 79.

China, a slave belonging to William Kemp, was born in August 1775 and was baptized on October 1, 1775. Kingston Parish Register, p. 83.

China, a slave belonging to William Kemp, was born in September 1775 and was baptized on November 12, 1775. Kingston Parish Register, p. 83.

China, a slave belonging to Humphrey Davis, was born in March 1776 and was baptized on June 16, 1776. Kingston Parish Register, p. 85.

China, a slave belonging to Anna Billups, was born in late 1776 or early 1777 and was baptized on February 23, 1777. Kingston Parish Register, p. 87.

China, a slave belonging to Edward Davis, was born on November 15, 1781. Kingston Parish Register, p. 89.

Chiney, a slave belonging to Kemp Whiting, was born in March 1757. Kingston Parish Register, p. 48.

Christian, a female slave belonging to Robert Billups, was born on April 15, 1764. Kingston Parish Register, p. 58.

Christian, a slave belonging to John Billups, was born on December 20, 1769. Kingston Parish Register, p. 66.

Christian, a female slave belonging to Bristow's estate, was born in March 1771 and was baptized on April 14, 1771. Kingston Parish Register, p. 67.

Christianity, a slave belonging to William Armistead, was baptized on April 1, 1750. Kingston Parish Register, p. 41.

Christopher, a slave belonging to Dawson Eddins, was born on March 20, 1775, and was baptized on May 7, 1775. Kingston Parish Register, p. 81.

Christopher, a slave belonging to Henry Knight, was born in late 1776 or early 1777 and was baptized on February 9, 1777. Kingston Parish Register, p. 87.

Clara, a slave belonging to Charles Burton, was born in March 1777 and was baptized on April 6, 1777. Kingston Parish Register, p. 87.

Clarinda, a slave belonging to John Keys, was born in March 1771 and was baptized on April 21, 1771. Kingston Parish Register, p. 67.

Clarinda, a slave belonging to John Keys, was baptized on April 21, 1771. Kingston Parish Register, p. 70.

Clem, a slave belonging to Mrs. Mary Cunningham, was born on July 8, 1747. Kingston Parish Register, p. 103.

Cleopatra, a slave girl belonging to Capt. Gwyn Read, was born on January 9, 1754. Kingston Parish Register, p. 45.

Collier, Peyton. See Peyton Collier.

Comer, a slave belonging to Robert Green, was born in March 1774 and was baptized on April 10, 1774. Kingston Parish Register, p. 77.

Cooter, Thomas. See Thomas Cooter.

Cubit or Cubbat, a slave belonging to Mrs. Mary Cunningham, was born on October 20, 1748. Kingston Parish Register, p. 103.

Cuff, a slave belonging to Mary Lowry, was born in September or October 1776 and was baptized on December 15, 1776. Kingston Parish Register, p. 86.

Cuffy, a slave belonging to Major Kemp Plummer, was born on June 19, 1767. Kingston Parish Register, p. 63.

Cullifer, an adult slave belonging to Robert Spencer, was baptized on September 25, 1774. Kingston Parish Register, p. 79.

Currel, a slave belonging to William Hayes, was born on October 13, 1758. Kingston Parish Register, p. 50.

Currel, a slave belonging to Elizabeth Billups, was born on June 11, 1760. Kingston Parish Register, p. 52.

Currel, an adult slave belonging to [no first name] Lewis's estate, was baptized in 1772. Kingston Parish Register, p. 69.

Currel, a slave belonging to Major William Plummer, was born in May 1773 and was baptized on August 29, 1773. Kingston Parish Register, p. 76.

Currel, a slave belonging to Thomas Hayes, was born in March 1776 and was baptized on June 16, 1776. Kingston Parish Register, p. 85.

Cyrus, a slave belonging to the Honorable John Page of Ware Parish, was born in February 1773 and was baptized on May 16, 1773. Kingston Parish Register, p. 74.

D

Dan, a slave belonging to Capt. George Dudley, was baptized on April 16, 1750. Kingston Parish Register, p. 41.

Dan, a slave belonging to Robert Billups, was born on September 21, 1755. Kingston Parish Register, p. 46.

Dan, a slave belonging to John Newell, was born on June 20, 1756. Kingston Parish Register, p. 47.

Dan, a slave belonging to William Tompkins, was born in January 1763. Kingston Parish Register, p. 56.

Dan, a slave belonging to Elizabeth Lux, was born on August 4, 1774, and was baptized on August 28, 1774. Kingston Parish Register, p. 78.

Daniel, a slave belonging to Capt. George Dudley, was baptized on April 16, 1750. Kingston Parish Register, p. 41.

Daniel, a slave belonging to Capt. George Dudley, was baptized on April 16, 1750. Kingston Parish Register, p. 41.

Daniel, a slave belonging to Letitia Ransone, was baptized on September 30, 1750. Kingston Parish Register, p. 42.

Daniel, a slave belonging to Letitia Ránsone, was born in March 1758. Kingston Parish Register, p. 49.

Daniel, a slave belonging to Joseph Pritchard, was born on April 8, 1760. Kingston Parish Register, p. 52.

Daniel, a slave belonging to William Hayes, was born on January 25, 1761. Kingston Parish Register, p. 53.

Daniel, a slave belonging to Capt. Thomas Smith, was born on March 23, 1762. Kingston Parish Register, p. 55.

Daniel, a slave belonging to Margaret Machen, was born on November 25, 1764. Kingston Parish Register, p. 59.

Daniel, a slave belonging to Mary Blacknall, was born on February 11, 1766. Kingston Parish Register, p. 61.

Daniel, a slave belonging to John Davis, was born in July 1768. Kingston Parish Register, p. 65.

Daniel, a slave belonging to Gabriel Miller, was born in October 1768. Kingston Parish Register, p. 65.

Daniel, a slave belonging to Capt. William Hayes, was born on January 30, 1769. Kingston Parish Register, p. 65.

Daniel, a slave belonging to John Hayes, was born on January 25, 1772, and was baptized on March 1, 1772. Kingston Parish Register, p. 69.

Daniel, a slave belonging to Charles Jones, was baptized on June 16, 1772. Kingston Parish Register, p. 70.

Daniel, a slave belonging to George Alexander Dudley, was baptized on June 31, 1772. Kingston Parish Register, p. 70.

Daniel, a slave belonging to Thomas Billups, was born on April 7, 1773, and was baptized on May 9, 1773. Kingston Parish Register, p. 73.

Daniel, a slave belonging to John Page Esq. of Ware Parish, was born in June 1773 and was baptized on July 11, 1773. Kingston Parish Register, p. 75.

Daniel, a slave belonging to Robert Matthews, was born in August 1774 and was baptized on October 30, 1774. Kingston Parish Register, p. 79.

Daniel, a slave belonging to Frances Tabb, was born in March 1775 and was baptized on April 2, 1775. Kingston Parish Register, p. 81.

Daniel, a slave belonging to Dorothy Dudley, was born on April 3, 1777, and was baptized on June 1, 1777. Kingston Parish Register, p. 87.

Daniel Park, a slave belonging to Thomas James, was born on February 6, 1821. Kingston Parish Register, p. 90.

Daphne, a slave belonging to Mr. Ransone, was baptized on June 24, 1750. Kingston Parish Register, p. 42.

David, a slave belonging to William Tabb, was baptized on May 13, 1750. Kingston Parish Register, p. 42.

David, a slave belonging to Bristow's estate, was born in November 1756. Kingston Parish Register, p. 47.

David, a slave belonging to Joseph Gayle, was born on March 31, 1766. Kingston Parish Register, p. 61.

David, a slave belonging to Daniel Fitchett, was born on April 30, 1773, and was baptized on June 20, 1773. Kingston Parish Register, p. 74.

David, a slave belonging to Rose Hunley, was born on June 24, 1773, and was baptized on August 1, 1733. Kingston Parish Register, p. 75.

Davy, a slave belonging to John Eddins, was born on January 26, 1769. Kingston Parish Register, p. 65.

Davy, a slave belonging to Anna Billups, was born in March 1773 and was baptized on May 9, 1773. Kingston Parish Register, p. 73.

Delia, a slave belonging to Edmund Custis, was born in March 1774 and was baptized on May 8, 1774. Kingston Parish Register, p. 77.

Dennis, an illegitimate mulatto child, was born to Mary White, a Caucasian, on February 1, 1807. Kingston Parish Register, p. 90.

Diana, a slave belonging to Robert Spencer, was born in March 1774 and was baptized on April 17, 1774. Kingston Parish Register, p. 77.

Diana, an adult slave belonging to William Merchant, was baptized on September 25, 1774. Kingston Parish Register, p. 79.

Dicey, a slave belonging to Matthias James, was born on April 29, 1770. Kingston Parish Register, p. 66.

Dicey, a slave belonging to Isaac Smith, was born in February 1773 and was baptized on March 9, 1773. Kingston Parish Register, p. 74.

Dicey, a slave belonging to Robert Spencer, was born in June 1775 and was baptized on July 30, 1775. Kingston Parish Register, p. 83.

Dick, a slave belonging to Capt. Robert Whiting, was born on November 26, 1752. Kingston Parish Register, p. 43.

Dick, a slave belonging to John Read's estate, was born on August 25, 1754. Kingston Parish Register, p. 45.

Dick, a slave belonging to John Hayes, was born on January 2, 1755. Kingston Parish Register, p. 46.

Dick, a slave belonging to Capt. Thomas Hayes, was born on October 10, 1758. Kingston Parish Register, p. 50.

Dick, a slave belonging to Christopher Gayle, was born on February 31, 1760. Kingston Parish Register, p. 52.

Dick, a slave belonging to Capt. Thomas Smith, was born on April 1, 1764. Kingston Parish Register, p. 58.

Dick, a slave belonging to John Gayle, was born on January 8, 1765. Kingston Parish Register, p. 60.

Dick, a slave belonging to James Ransone, was born on April 14, 1765. Kingston Parish Register, p. 60.

Dick, a slave belonging to Thomas Hayes, was born in February 1776 and was baptized on March 17, 1776. Kingston Parish Register, p. 84.

Dicky, a slave belonging to Josiah Foster, was born on October 17, 1768. Kingston Parish Register, p. 65.

Dicy, a slave girl belonging to Captain Thomas Hayes, was born on July 22, 1752. Kingston Parish Register, p. 43.

Dicy, a slave belonging to Anthony Digges, was born on August 5, 1764. Kingston Parish Register, p. 59.

Dinah, a slave belonging to George Keeble, died in January 1750. Kingston Parish Register, p. 179.

Dinah, a slave belonging to James Hayes, was born on January 15, 1752. Kingston Parish Register, p. 43.

Dinah, an adult slave belonging to Francis Tabb, was baptized on August 30, 1772. Kingston Parish Register, p. 72.

Dinah, a slave belonging to Dorothy Matthews, was born in August 1774 and was baptized on September 18, 1774. Kingston Parish Register, p. 79.

Dinah, a slave belonging to William Buckner, was born in February 1776 and was baptized on April 21, 1776. Kingston Parish Register, p. 84.

Doll, a slave belonging to James Ransone, was born on September 14, 1753. Kingston Parish Register, p. 44.

Doll, a slave belonging to William Hayes, was born on August 30, 1755. Kingston Parish Register, p. 46.

Doll, a slave belonging to Robert Billups, was born in March 1761. Kingston Parish Register, p. 54.

Doll, a slave belonging to John Davis, was born on August 15, 1762. Kingston Parish Register, p. 55.

Doll, a slave belonging to Major Kemp Plummer, was born on December 29, 1764. Kingston Parish Register, p. 59.

Dolly, a slave belonging to Letitia Ransone, was baptized on September 16, 1750. Kingston Parish Register, p. 42.

Dolly, a slave belonging to John Eddins, was born on August 30, 1771, and was baptized on October 13, 1771. Kingston Parish Register, p. 68.

Dolly, a slave belonging to Capt. Robert Billups, was born in October 1774 and was baptized on December 18, 1775. Kingston Parish Register, p. 80.

Dolly, a slave belonging to Henry Gwyn, was born in July 1776 and was baptized on July 28, 1776. Kingston Parish Register, p. 85.

Dorothy, a slave belonging to Letitia Ransone, was baptized on September 16, 1750. Kingston Parish Register, p. 42.

Dorothy, a slave belonging to Mann Page Esq., of Ware Parish, was born in December 1774 and was baptized on February 5, 1775. Kingston Parish Register, p. 80.

Dorothy, a slave belonging to Robert Bristow Esq., was born in March 1777 and was baptized on May 19, 1777. Kingston Parish Register, p. 87.

E

Easter, a slave belonging to Humphrey Billups, was born on November 24, 1757. Kingston Parish Register, p. 49.

Eddy, a slave belonging to the Rev. John Dixon, was born on May 5, 1766. Kingston Parish Register, p. 62.

Edmund, a slave belonging to Robert Spencer, was baptized on October 13, 1771. Kingston Parish Register, p. 68.

Edmund, a slave belonging to Robert Matthews, was born in September 1772 and was baptized on November 1, 1772. Kingston Parish Register, p. 71.

Edmund, an adult slave belonging to Langley Billups' widow, was baptized on July 4, 1773. Kingston Parish Register, p. 75.

Edmund, a slave belonging to Thomas Blake, was born in March 1774 and was baptized on April 10, 1774. Kingston Parish Register, p. 77.

Edmund, a slave belonging to Elizabeth Lux, was born in January 1775 and was baptized on March 12, 1775. Kingston Parish Register, p. 80.

Edmund, a slave belonging to John Elliott, was born in February 1777 and was baptized on March 16, 1777. Kingston Parish Register, p. 87.

Edmund, a slave belonging to Dorothy Cary, was born on April 3, 1777, and was baptized on June 1, 1777. Kingston Parish Register, p. 87.

Edward, a slave belonging to Rose Window's estate, was born on May 25, 1769. Kingston Parish Register, p. 52.

Eleanor, a slave belonging to John Roots, was born in August 1763. Kingston Parish Register, p. 57.

Eliza, a slave belonging to Humphrey Thomas, was born on July 18, 1756. Kingston Parish Register, p. 47.

Eliza, a slave belonging to Thomas James, was born in April 1803. Kingston Parish Register, p. 89.

Elizabeth, a slave belonging to Charles Blacknall, was born on November 4, 1759. Kingston Parish Register, p. 51.

Elizabeth, a slave belonging to the Widow Spencer, was baptized on March 25, 1750. Kingston Parish Register, p. 41.

Elizabeth, a slave belonging to James Hayes, was baptized on May 13, 1750. Kingston Parish Register, p. 42.

Elizabeth, a slave belonging to Mr. Smith, was baptized on May 13, 1750. Kingston Parish Register, p. 42.

Elizabeth, a slave belonging to Mr. Keeble, was baptized on June 10, 1750. Kingston Parish Register, p. 42.

Elizabeth, a slave belonging to John Armistead, was baptized on September 30, 1750. Kingston Parish Register, p. 42.

Elizabeth, a slave belonging to Robert Tompkins, was born in December 1770 and was baptized on March 17, 1771. Kingston Parish Register, p. 67.

Elizabeth, a slave belonging to Margaret Machen, was born in March 1774 and was baptized on May 8, 1774. Kingston Parish Register, p. 77.

Elizabeth, a slave belonging to John Machen, was born in 1776 and was baptized on March 10, 1776. Kingston Parish Register, p. 84.

Elizabeth, an adult slave belonging to Lukey Hudgins, was baptized on July 2, 1775. Kingston Parish Register, p. 82.

Elizabeth, a slave belonging to Walter Keeble, was born in March 1776 and was baptized on May 5, 1776. Kingston Parish Register, p. 85.

Ellinsone, a slave belonging to Thomas James, was born on June 1, 1827. Kingston Parish Register, p. 90.

Emanuel, a slave belonging to William Armistead Esq., was born in August 1774 and was baptized on October 30, 1774. Kingston Parish Register, p. 79.

Esop and Jacob, twin slaves belonging to Mary Plummer, were born on September 4, 1774, and were baptized on December 4, 1774. Kingston Parish Register, p. 80.

Essex, a slave belonging to Capt. Kemp Plummer, was born in May 1756. Kingston Parish Register, p. 47.

Esther, a slave belonging to John Davis, was born on July 15, 1764. Kingston Parish Register, p. 59.

Esther, a slave belonging to John Billups Jr., was born on March 26, 1766. Kingston Parish Register, p. 61.

Esther, a slave belonging to Gabriel Miller, was born on July 15, 1776. Kingston Parish Register, p. 62.

Esther, a slave belonging to George Forrest, was born on July 26, 1766. Kingston Parish Register, p. 62.

Esther, a slave belonging to Capt. Thomas Smith, was born on February 17, 1767. Kingston Parish Register, p. 63.

Esther, a slave belonging to John Respass, was born on July 29, 1770. Kingston Parish Register, p. 66.

Esther, a slave belonging to Christopher Brown, was born on December 11, 1770, and was baptized on August 4, 1771. Kingston Parish Register, p. 68.

Esther, a slave belonging to Dawson Eddins, was born on July 29, 1772, and was baptized on September 13, 1772. Kingston Parish Register, p. 71.

Esther, an adult slave belonging to John Callis, was baptized on July 3, 1773. Kingston Parish Register, p. 75.

Esther, a slave belonging to William Stewart or Stuart, was born on April 1, 1774, and was baptized on June 5, 1774. Kingston Parish Register, p. 78.

Esther, a slave belonging to John King, was born in August 1774 and was baptized on September 18, 1774. Kingston Parish Register, p. 79.

Esther, a slave belonging to Robert Spencer, was born in September 1774 and was baptized on December 11, 1774. Kingston Parish Register, p. 80.

Esther, a slave belonging to Sir John Peyton, was born in July 1776 and was baptized on August 4, 1776. Kingston Parish Register, p. 86.

Esther and Grace, twin slaves belonging to Edward Hughes, were born on July 14, 1776, and were baptized on July 28, 1776. Kingston Parish Register, p. 85.

Esther, a slave belonging to Elizabeth Jones, was born in late 1776 or early 1777 and was baptized on February 2, 1777. Kingston Parish Register, p. 87.

Eve, a slave belonging to Capt. Read, was baptized on September 16, 1750. Kingston Parish Register, p. 42.

Eve, a slave girl belonging to Gwyn Read, was born on May 29, 1752. Kingston Parish Register, p. 43.

Eve, a slave belonging to John Roots, was born on October 4, 1761. Kingston Parish Register, p. 54.

Eve, a slave belonging to Milly Read, was born on July 14, 1774, and was baptized on August 28, 1774. Kingston Parish Register, p. 78.

Eve, a slave belonging to John Dixon, was born in December 1774 and was baptized on February 5, 1775. Kingston Parish Register, p. 80.

Eve, a slave belonging to Capt. John Billups, was born on March 27, 1775, and was baptized on May 7, 1775. Kingston Parish Register, p. 81.

Eve, a slave belonging to George Armistead, was born on June 6, 1775, and was baptized on July 16, 1775. Kingston Parish Register, p. 82.

F

Fanny, a slave belonging to John Cary Jr., was born on June 20, 1753. Kingston Parish Register, p. 44.

Fanny, a slave belonging to Mrs. Anna Armistead, was born on April 10, 1755. Kingston Parish Register, p. 46.

Fanny, a slave belonging to William Hayes, was born May 10, 1756. Kingston Parish Register, p. 47.

Fanny, a slave belonging to James Ransone, was born on May 20, 1756. Kingston Parish Register, p. 47.

Fanny, a slave belonging to James Ransone, was born on June 20, 1756. Kingston Parish Register, p. 47. *Note: this register entry was crossed out.*

Fanny, a slave belonging to John Hayes, was born on October 12, 1759. Kingston Parish Register, p. 51.

Fanny, a slave belonging to Elizabeth Holder, was born on March 22, 1761. Kingston Parish Register, p. 54.

Fanny, a slave belonging to Elizabeth Green, was born on March 20, 1763. Kingston Parish Register, p. 56.

Fanny, a slave belonging to Capt. Thomas Smith, was born on April 9, 1767. Kingston Parish Register, p. 63.

Fanny, a slave belonging to Major William Plummer, was born on June 19, 1767. Kingston Parish Register, p. 63.

Fanny, a slave belonging to Lucy Machen, was born in January 1768. Kingston Parish Register, p. 64.

Fanny, a slave belonging to Christopher Gayle, was born on January 1, 1768. Kingston Parish Register, p. 64.

Fanny, a slave belonging to Capt. Thomas Hayes, was born on December 18, 1768. Kingston Parish Register, p. 65.

Fanny, a slave belonging to the Rev. John Dixon, was born on February 10, 1769. Kingston Parish Register, p. 65.

Fanny, a slave belonging to Richard Foster, was born on February 16, 1769. Kingston Parish Register, p. 65.

Fanny, a slave belonging to Robert Hunley, was born on September 8, 1769, and was baptized on October 27, 1771. Kingston Parish Register, p. 68.

Fanny, a female slave belonging to Mrs. Mary Blacknall, was born on March 7, 1771, and was baptized on April 14, 1771. Kingston Parish Register, p. 67.

Fanny, a slave belonging to George William Plummer, was born on August 6, 1771, and was baptized on September 1, 1771. Kingston Parish Register, p. 68.

Fanny, a slave belonging to Margaret Machen, was born on January 12, 1772, and was baptized on March 1, 1772. Kingston Parish Register, p. 69.

Fanny, a slave belonging to Capt. Francis Armistead, was born on September 12, 1773, and was baptized on October 24, 1773. Kingston Parish Register, p. 76.

Fanny, a slave belonging to Joyce Davis, was born on March 5, 1774, and was baptized on June 5, 1774. Kingston Parish Register, p. 78.

Fanny, a slave belonging to Walter Keeble, was born in August 1774 and was baptized on September 18, 1774. Kingston Parish Register, p. 79.

Fanny, a slave belonging to Susanna Tabb, was born in March 1775 and was baptized on August 6, 1775. Kingston Parish Register, p. 83.

Fanny, a slave belonging to John Foster, was born in July 1775 and was baptized on July 16, 1775. Kingston Parish Register, p. 83.

Fanny, a slave belonging to John Foster, was baptized on July 16, 1775. Kingston Parish Register, p. 83.

Fanny, a slave belonging to John Machen, was born in July 1775 and was baptized on August 27, 1775. Kingston Parish Register, p. 83.

Fanny, a slave belonging to Frances Tabb, was born in August 1775 and was baptized on October 15, 1775. Kingston Parish Register, p. 83.

Fanny, a slave belonging to William Lilly, was born in October 1775 and was baptized on December 17, 1775. Kingston Parish Register, p. 83.

Fanny, a slave belonging to Harry Gwyn, was born in February 1776 and was baptized on March 10, 1776. Kingston Parish Register, p. 84.

Fanny, a slave belonging to Peter Bernard, was born in July 1776 and was baptized on August 4, 1776. Kingston Parish Register, p. 86.

Fanny, a slave belonging to Thomas Poole, was born in September or October 1776 and was baptized on December 29, 1776. Kingston Parish Register, p. 86.

Fanny, a slave belonging to John Elliott, was born in February 1777 and was baptized on March 16, 1777. Kingston Parish Register, p. 87.

Fanny, a slave belonging to John Billups, was born in April 1777 and was baptized on June 1, 1777. Kingston Parish Register, p. 88.

Fanny, a slave child belonging to Isaac Foster, was baptized on July 16, 1775. Kingston Parish Register, p. 82.

Fitchet, a slave belonging to William Merchant, was born in March 1775 and was baptized on April 30, 1775. Kingston Parish Register, p. 81.

Floro, a slave belonging to Joel Foster, was born on January 22, 1769. Kingston Parish Register, p. 65.

Fluky, a slave belonging to Major Kemp Plummer, was born on March 16, 1768. Kingston Parish Register, p. 64.

Frances, a 24-year-old slave associated with the Kingston Parish glebe, was baptized on November 26, 1749. Kingston Parish Register, p. 41.

Frances, a slave belonging to John Foster, was born on April 3, 1769. Kingston Parish Register, p. 65.

Francis, a slave belonging to William Gwyn, was baptized on May 6, 1750. Kingston Parish Register, p. 41.

Francis, a slave belonging to William Armistead Esq., was born in February 1773 and was baptized on May 2, 1773. Kingston Parish Register, p. 74.

Frank, a slave belonging to William Hayes, was born on January 17, 1754. Kingston Parish Register, p. 45.

Frank, a slave belonging to Thomas Brooks, was born on September 14, 1760. Kingston Parish Register, p. 53.

Frank, a slave belonging to John Hayes, was born on January 12, 1762. Kingston Parish Register, p. 55.

Frank, a slave belonging to Christopher Gayle, was born on June 8, 1766. Kingston Parish Register, p. 62.

Frank, a slave belonging to Robert Tompkins, was born in March 1767. Kingston Parish Register, p. 63.

Frank Sprig, a slave belonging to Tinsley or Tindsley Dixon, was born in April 1770. Kingston Parish Register, p. 66.

Frank, a slave belonging to John Willis, was born on February 14, 1771, and was baptized in August 1771. Kingston Parish Register, p. 68.

Frank, a slave boy belonging to John Willis, was born on February 14, 1771, and was baptized on April 14, 1771. Kingston Parish Register, p. 67.

Frank, a female slave belonging to Major William Plummer, was born in April 1771 and was baptized on June 9, 1771. Kingston Parish Register, p. 67.

Frank, an adult female slave belonging to John Samson, was baptized on October 5, 1771. Kingston Parish Register, p. 68.

Frank, an adult female slave belonging to William Hunley, was baptized on August 30, 1772. Kingston Parish Register, p. 72.

Frank, a slave belonging to William Lilly, was born on May 13, 1773, and was baptized on July 4, 1773. Kingston Parish Register, p. 75.

Frank, a slave belonging to Joseph Billups, was born on August 29, 1773, and was baptized on October 24, 1773. Kingston Parish Register, p. 76.

Frank, a slave belonging to Mary Hayes, was born in September 1773 and was baptized on October 24, 1773. Kingston Parish Register, p. 76.

Frank, a slave girl belonging to Mrs. Judith Plummer, was born in April 1774 and was baptized on March 13, 1774. Kingston Parish Register, p. 77.

Frank, a slave belonging to George William Plummer, was born in October 1775 and was baptized on December 17, 1775. Kingston Parish Register, p. 83.

Franky or Frankey, a slave belonging to Charles Blacknall, was born on July 27, 1760. Kingston Parish Register, p. 52.

Franky or Frankey, a slave belonging to Francis Armistead, was born on September 16, 1763. Kingston Parish Register, p. 57.

Franky or Frankey, a slave belonging to John Roots, was born on May 23, 1766. Kingston Parish Register, p. 62.

Franky, a slave belonging to John Eddins, was born in February 1770. Kingston Parish Register, p. 66.

Franky or Frankey, a slave belonging to James Davis, was born on April 15, 1770. Kingston Parish Register, p. 66.

Franky, a female slave belonging to Mrs. Mary Blacknall, was born on March 7, 1771, and was baptized on April 14, 1771. Kingston Parish Register, p. 67.

Franky, a slave belonging to Jasper Clayton of Ware Parish, was born in February 1773 and was baptized on April 4, 1773. Kingston Parish Register, p. 73.

Franky, a slave belonging to Dorothy Cary, was born on June 5, 1773, and was baptized on September 5, 1773. Kingston Parish Register, p. 76.

Franky, a slave belonging to John Hayes, was born on October 30, 1774, and was baptized on December 18, 1775. Kingston Parish Register, p. 80.

Franky, a slave belonging to George Fitzhugh, was born in July 1776 and was baptized on August 4, 1776. Kingston Parish Register, p. 86.

Franky, a slave belonging to John Armistead's estate, was born on August 3, 1776, and was baptized on September 22, 1776. Kingston Parish Register, p. 86.

G

Gabriel, a slave belonging to Richard Hunley, was baptized on September 2, 1750. Kingston Parish Register, p. 42.

Gabriel, a slave belonging to John Gwyn, was born on August 9, 1757. Kingston Parish Register, p. 48.

Gabriel, a slave belonging to Robert Tompkins, was born on July 22, 1764. Kingston Parish Register, p. 59.

Gabriel, a slave belonging to Lucretia Lewis, was born on January 13, 1771, and was baptized on March 17, 1771. Kingston Parish Register, p. 70.

Gabriel, a slave belonging to the Honorable John Page Esq., of Ware Parish, was baptized on May 5, 1771. Kingston Parish Register, p. 70.

Gabriel, a slave belonging to John Gayle, was born in August 1772 and was baptized on September 13, 1772. Kingston Parish Register, p. 71.

Gabriel, a slave belonging to John Callis, was born in August 1775 and was baptized on August 27, 1775. Kingston Parish Register, p. 83.

Gabriel, a slave belonging to Samuel Eddins, was born in March 1776 and was baptized on June 16, 1776. Kingston Parish Register, p. 85.

George, a slave belonging to Letitia Ransone, was baptized on September 16, 1750. Kingston Parish Register, p. 42.

George, a slave belonging to Thomas Hayes Jr., was born on June 22, 1756. Kingston Parish Register, p. 47.

George, a slave belonging to Thomas Forrest, was born in November 1756. Kingston Parish Register, p.47.

George, a slave belonging to John Lilly, was born in March 1757. Kingston Parish Register, p. 48.

George, a slave belonging to Francis Digges, was born in December 1760. Kingston Parish Register, p. 53.

George, a slave belonging to John Billups Jr., was born in May 1763. Kingston Parish Register, p. 57.

George, a slave belonging to John Davis, was born on April 4, 1764. Kingston Parish Register, p. 58.

George, a slave belonging to James Harper, was born in December 1767. Kingston Parish Register, p. 64.

George, a slave belonging to James Davis, was born on April 17, 1770. Kingston Parish Register, p. 66.

George, a slave belonging to Major Kemp Plummer, was born in July 1770. Kingston Parish Register, p. 66.

George, a slave belonging to William Plummer, was born on November 4, 1770. Kingston Parish Register, p. 66.

George, a slave belonging to John Armistead, was born on November 16, 1770, and was baptized on January 6, 1771. Kingston Parish Register, p. 67.

George, a slave belonging to John Read, was born on September 6, 1771, and was baptized on October 13, 1771. Kingston Parish Register, p. 68.

George, a slave belonging to Capt. Robert Billups, was born on December 11, 1771, and was baptized on January 5, 1772. Kingston Parish Register, p. 69.

George, an adult slave belonging to the Widow Hunley, was baptized in 1772. Kingston Parish Register, p. 69.

George, an adult slave belonging to Matthias James, was baptized on August 30, 1772. Kingston Parish Register, p. 72.

George, a slave belonging to Gabriel Hughes, was born in February 1773 and was baptized on May 2, 1773. Kingston Parish Register, p. 74.

George, a slave belonging to James Davis, was born on May 9, 1773, and was baptized on July 4, 1773. Kingston Parish Register, p. 75.

George, a slave belonging to Isaac Smith, was born on December 25, 1774, and was baptized on February 26, 1775. Kingston Parish Register, p. 80.

George, a slave belonging to Edmund Borum Sr., was born in July 1776 and was baptized on September 8, 1776. Kingston Parish Register, p. 86.

George, a slave belonging to Margaret Machen, was born in August 1776 and was baptized on October 20, 1776. Kingston Parish Register, p. 86.

George, an adult slave belonging to the widow Dorothy Dudley, was baptized on May 19, 1777. Kingston Parish Register, p. 87.

George, a slave belonging to Robert Hunley, was born in June 1777 and was baptized on August 10, 1777. Kingston Parish Register, p. 88.

Gibson, a slave belonging to Hugh Hudgins, was born in September 1772 and was baptized on November 1, 1772. Kingston Parish Register, p. 71.

Gilly, a slave belonging to Richard Merchant, was born in January 1757. Kingston Parish Register, p. 48.

Gingo, a slave belonging to James Callis, was baptized on January 24, 1747. Kingston Parish Register, p. 42.

Grace, a slave belonging to Thomas Machen or Michen, was baptized on July 24, 1747. Kingston Parish Register, p. 42.

Grace, a slave belonging to James Peade, was born on September 2, 1767. Kingston Parish Register, p. 63.

Grace, a slave belonging to James Davis, was born on April 7, 1768. Kingston Parish Register, p. 64.

Grace, a slave belonging to John Foster, was born on April 7, 1769. Kingston Parish Register, p.65.

Grace, a slave belonging to Edmund Custis, was born on February 7, 1772, and was baptized on July 5, 1772. Kingston Parish Register, p. 69.

Grace, a slave belonging to Sir John Peyton, was born in February 1773 and was baptized on May 16, 1773. Kingston Parish Register, p. 74.

Grace, an adult slave belonging to John King, was baptized on September 25, 1774. Kingston Parish Register, p. 79.

Grace, a slave belonging to William Merchant, was born in March 1775 and was baptized on April 2, 1775. Kingston Parish Register, p. 81.

Grace, a slave belonging to Gabriel Hughes, was born in July 1776 and was baptized on September 8, 1776. Kingston Parish Register, p. 86.

Grace and Esther, twin slaves belonging to Edward Hughes, were born on July 14, 1776, and were baptized on July 19, 1776. Kingston Parish Register, p. 85.

Grace, a slave belonging to Hannah Tompkins, was born in September or October 1776 and was baptized on December 15, 1776. Kingston Parish Register, p. 86.

Grace, a slave belonging to John Dixon, was born in February 1777 and was baptized on April 11, 1777. Kingston Parish Register, p. 87.

Green, Sparkley. See Sparkley Green.

Guy, a slave belonging to Dorothy Cary, was born in October 1772 and was baptized on December 13, 1772. Kingston Parish Register, p. 71.

H

Hannah, a slave belonging to John Read, was baptized on April 29, 1750. Kingston Parish Register, p. 41.

Hannah, a slave belonging to William Hayes, was baptized on September 2, 1750. Kingston Parish Register, p. 42.

Hannah, a slave belonging to Mrs. Cunningham, was baptized on September 30, 1750. Kingston Parish Register, p. 42.

Hannah, a slave girl belonging to Joseph Davis, was born on June 10, 1751. Kingston Parish Register, p. 43.

Hannah, a slave belonging to Richard Merchant, was born on November 4, 1753. Kingston Parish Register, p. 45.

Hannah, a slave belonging to John Gwyn, was born on August 13, 1754. Kingston Parish Register, p. 45.

Hannah, a slave belonging to Charles Blacknall, was born on September 25, 1756. Kingston Parish Register, p. 47.

Hannah, a slave belonging to Mary Dunbar, was born in September 1757. Kingston Parish Register, p. 49.

Hannah, a slave belonging to Richard Merchant, was born on June 1, 1758. Kingston Parish Register, p. 49.

Hannah, a slave belonging to John Eddins, was born on August 31, 1758. Kingston Parish Register, p. 50.

Hannah, a slave belonging to Harry Gwyn, was born on June 5, 1759. Kingston Parish Register, p. 51.

Hannah, a slave belonging to William Hayes, was born on March 1, 1761. Kingston Parish Register, p. 54.

Hannah, a slave belonging to John Hayes, was born on April 21, 1763. Kingston Parish Register, p. 57.

Hannah, a slave belonging to George Turner, was born on June 19, 1763. Kingston Parish Register, p. 57.

Hannah, a slave belonging to Matthias James, was born on August 26, 1763. Kingston Parish Register, p. 57.

Hannah, a slave belonging to Francis Armistead, was born on May 11, 1764. Kingston Parish Register, p. 58.

Hannah, a slave belonging to Elizabeth Billups, was born on November 4, 1764. Kingston Parish Register, p. 59.

Hannah, a slave belonging to John Cary Jr., was born on May 16, 1765. Kingston Parish Register, p. 60.

Hannah, a slave belonging to Capt. William Hayes, was born on November 23, 1765. Kingston Parish Register, p. 61.

Hannah, a slave belonging to Capt. William Hayes, was born on August 25, 1766. Kingston Parish Register, p. 62.

Hannah, a slave belonging to Humphrey Billups, was born in January 1767. Kingston Parish Register, p. 63.

Hannah, a slave belonging to John Billups, was born on January 17, 1768. Kingston Parish Register, p. 64.

Hannah, a slave belonging to John Hurst, was born on June 2, 1768. Kingston Parish Register, p. 65.

Hannah, a slave belonging to Rose Lilly, was born on June 18, 1768. Kingston Parish Register, p. 65.

Hannah, a slave belonging to Richard Gwyn, was born on November 11, 1768. Kingston Parish Register, p. 65.

Hannah, a slave belonging to Lucy Palmer, was born on February 19, 1769. Kingston Parish Register, p. 65.

Hannah, an adult slave belonging to Currel Armistead, was baptized on August 30, 1772. Kingston Parish Register, p. 72.

Hannah, a slave belonging to Richard Brooks, was born in February 1773 and was baptized on May 9, 1773. Kingston Parish Register, p. 73.

Hannah, a slave belonging to Samuel Eddins, was born in January 1774 and was baptized on February 27, 1774. Kingston Parish Register, p. 77.

Hannah, a slave belonging to John Hayes, was born on July 17, 1774, and was baptized on August 28, 1774. Kingston Parish Register, p. 78.

Hannah, a slave belonging to Edward Anderson, was born in May 1775 and was baptized on July 2, 1775. Kingston Parish Register, p. 82.

Hannah, a slave belonging to Frances Tabb, was born in May 1775 and was baptized on July 9, 1775. Kingston Parish Register, p. 82.

Hannah, a slave belonging to Jasper Clayton of Ware Parish, was born in September 1775 and was baptized on November 12, 1775. Kingston Parish Register, p. 83.

Hannah, a slave belonging to John Callis, was born in March 1776 and was baptized on June 16, 1776. Kingston Parish Register, p. 85.

Hannah, a slave belonging to John Callis, was born in July 1776, and was baptized on August 25, 1776. Kingston Parish Register, p. 86.

Hannah, a slave belonging to Thomas Hudgins, was born in August 1776 and was baptized on September 29, 1776. Kingston Parish Register, p. 86.

Hannah, a slave belonging to Betty Jarvis, was born in August 1776 and was baptized on October 20, 1776. Kingston Parish Register, p. 86.

Hannah, a slave belonging to Major Thomas Smith, was born in August 1776 and was baptized on October 20, 1776. Kingston Parish Register, p. 86.

Hannah, a slave belonging to William Buckner, was born in November 1776 and was baptized on January 23, 1777. Kingston Parish Register, p. 87.

Hannah, a slave belonging to Robert Billups, was born in March 1777 and was baptized on May 4, 1777. Kingston Parish Register, p. 87.

Hannah, a slave girl belonging to Thomas James, was born on October 4, 1797. Kingston Parish Register, p. 89.

Harry, a slave belonging to George Keeble, was baptized on April 16, 1750. Kingston Parish Register, p. 41.

Harry, a slave belonging to Capt. George Dudley, was baptized on April 16, 1750. Kingston Parish Register, p. 41.

Harry, a slave belonging to William Bond, was born on September 2, 1753. Kingston Parish Register, p. 44.

Harry, a slave belonging to Edward Borum, was born on June 20, 1758. Kingston Parish Register, p. 47.

Harry, a slave belonging to Thomas Smith, was born on December 27, 1758. Kingston Parish Register, p. 50.

Harry, a slave belonging to James Harper, was born on January 6, 1760. Kingston Parish Register, p. 52.

Harry, a slave belonging to Ann Brooks, was born on May 21, 1760. Kingston Parish Register, p. 52.

Harry, a slave belonging to Wilkinson Hunley, was born on July 20, 1760. Kingston Parish Register, p. 52.

Harry, a slave belonging to John Hewell, was born on June 15, 1762. Kingston Parish Register, p. 55.

Harry, a slave belonging to Edward Davis, was born on April 24, 1763. Kingston Parish Register, p. 57.

Harry, a slave belonging to Major Kemp Plummer, was born in September 1765. Kingston Parish Register, p. 61.

Harry, a slave belonging to Josiah Foster, was born on July 30, 1767. Kingston Parish Register, p. 63.

Harry, a slave belonging to William Minter, was born on September 21, 1769. Kingston Parish Register, p. 66.

Harry, a slave belonging to John Eddins, was born on September 16, 1770. Kingston Parish Register, p. 66.

Harry, a slave belonging to Currel Armistead, was born on May 2, 1771, and was baptized on June 23, 1771. Kingston Parish Register, p. 68.

Harry and Bob, twin slaves belonging to John Eddins Jr., were born on June 21, 1772, and were baptized on July 5, 1772. Kingston Parish Register, p. 69.

Harry, a slave belonging to Judith Plummer, was born on July 4, 1773, and was baptized on August 29, 1773. Kingston Parish Register, p. 76.

Harry, a slave belonging to Joshua Foster, was born in October 1773 and was baptized on December 5, 1773. Kingston Parish Register, p. 76.

Harry, a slave belonging to Judith Plummer, was born in January 1775 and was baptized on March 19, 1775. Kingston Parish Register, p. 80.

Harry, a slave belonging to Joseph Davis, was born on February 24, 1775, and was baptized on April 9, 1775. Kingston Parish Register, p. 81.

Harry, a slave belonging to William Lilly, was born in April 1777 and was baptized on June 1, 1777. Kingston Parish Register, p. 88.

Haty, a slave belonging to Richard Hunley, was baptized on March 13, 1750. Kingston Parish Register, p. 42.

Hega, a slave belonging to Gabriel Miller, was born on August 4, 1799. Kingston Parish Register, p. 89.

Henry, a slave belonging to Mr. Debman, was baptized on March 11, 1750. Kingston Parish Register, p. 41.

Henry, a slave belonging to William Armistead, was baptized on April 1, 1750. Kingston Parish Register, p. 41.

Henry, a slave belonging to Thomas Machen or Michen, was baptized on May 20, 1750. Kingston Parish Register, p. 42.

Henry, a slave boy belonging to Ann Armistead, was born on December 3, 1752. Kingston Parish Register, p. 43.

Henry, a slave belonging to Edward Davis, was born in February 1763. Kingston Parish Register, p. 56.

Henry, a slave belonging to Thomas Poole, was born on June 23, 1764. Kingston Parish Register, p. 59.

Henry, a slave belonging to Mary Blacknall, was born on January 2, 1769. Kingston Parish Register, p. 65.

Henry, a slave belonging to Capt. Thomas Smith, was born on August 11, 1772, and was baptized on September 13, 1772. Kingston Parish Register, p. 71.

Henry, a slave belonging to Robert Read, was born in May 1773 and was baptized on September 26, 1773. Kingston Parish Register, p. 76.

Henry, a slave belonging to Joseph Billups, was born on October 11, 1773, and was baptized on November 11, 1773. Kingston Parish Register, p. 76.

Henry, an adult slave belonging to Mr. Borum, was baptized on September 25, 1774. Kingston Parish Register, p. 79.

Henry, a slave belonging to Susanna Tabb, was born in March 1775 and was baptized on April 2, 1775. Kingston Parish Register, p. 81.

Henry, a slave belonging to Thomas Iverson, was born in late 1775 or early 1776 and was baptized on January 21, 1776. Kingston Parish Register, p. 84.

Henry, a slave belonging to John Tompkins' estate, was born in late 1775 or early 1776 and was baptized on January 21, 1776. Kingston Parish Register, p. 84.

Henry, a slave belonging to Thomas James, was born on May 1, 1808. Kingston Parish Register, p. 90.

Hester, a slave belonging to Richard Billups, was baptized on April 1, 1750. Kingston Parish Register, p. 41.

Hester, a slave belonging to Major Dudley, was baptized on April 29, 1750. Kingston Parish Register, p. 41.

Hester, a slave belonging to William Hayes, was baptized on September 2, 1750. Kingston Parish Register, p. 42.

Hester, a slave belonging to William Tabb, was baptized on September 9, 1750. Kingston Parish Register, p. 42.

Hester, a slave belonging to Letitia Ransone, was baptized on September 16, 1750. Kingston Parish Register, p. 42.

Hester, a slave belonging to Daniel Williams, was born on November 8, 1755. Kingston Parish Register, p. 46.

Hester, a slave belonging to Catherine Miller, was born in July 1757. Kingston Parish Register, p. 48.

Hester, a slave belonging to John Lilly, was born on March 5, 1760. Kingston Parish Register, p. 52.

Howe, William. See William Howe.

Hugh, a slave belonging to John Tabb, was born in August 1773 and was baptized on December 12, 1773. Kingston Parish Register, p. 76.

Hukey, a slave belonging to Mary Digges, was born in March 1777 and was baptized on May 4, 1777. Kingston Parish Register, p. 87.

Humphrey or Humphry, a slave belonging to Hugh Gwyn, was born on April 1, 1750. Kingston Parish Register, p. 103.

Humphrey, a slave boy belonging to Captain Gwyn Read, was born on March 17, 1753. Kingston Parish Register, p. 44.

Humphrey, a slave belonging to John Cary Jr., was born on April 21, 1762. Kingston Parish Register, p. 57.

Humphrey, a slave belonging to William Plummer, was born on January 1, 1764. Kingston Parish Register, p. 58.

Humphrey, a slave belonging to Kemp Plummer, was born in July 1764. Kingston Parish Register, p. 59.

Humphrey, a slave belonging to Capt. Robert Billups, was born on June 20, 1767. Kingston Parish Register, p. 63.

Humphrey, a slave belonging to James Peade, was born on February 10, 1770. Kingston Parish Register, p. 66.

Humphrey, a slave belonging to Joshua Foster, was born in February 1771 and was baptized on June 9, 1771. Kingston Parish Register, p. 67.

Humphrey, a slave belonging to William Stewart or Stuart, was born on April 25, 1771, and was baptized on June 23, 1771. Kingston Parish Register, p. 68.

Humphrey, a slave belonging to Robert Green, was baptized on June 31, 1772. Kingston Parish Register, p. 70.

Humphrey, an adult slave belonging to James Hunley, was baptized on August 30, 1772. Kingston Parish Register, p. 72.

Humphrey, a slave belonging to Augustine Curtis, was born in late 1772 or early 1773 and was baptized on February 7, 1773. Kingston Parish Register, p. 73.

Humphrey, a slave belonging to Thomas Poole, was born in September 1774 and was baptized on December 11, 1774. Kingston Parish Register, p. 80.

I

Isaac, a slave belonging to Mr. Brooks' estate, was baptized on April 1, 1750. Kingston Parish Register, p. 41.

Isaac, a slave belonging to James Ransone's estate, was baptized on April 16, 1750. Kingston Parish Register, p. 41.

Isaac, a slave belonging to Major Dudley, was baptized on April 29, 1750. Kingston Parish Register, p. 41.

Isaac, a slave belonging to Thomas Machen or Michen, was baptized on May 20, 1750. Kingston Parish Register, p. 42.

Isaac, a slave belonging to John Cary Sr., was born on July 21, 1753. Kingston Parish Register, p. 44.

Isaac, a slave belonging to Capt. William Plummer, was born on March 2, 1757. Kingston Parish Register, p. 48.

Isaac, a slave belonging to John Hayes, was born on December 29, 1757. Kingston Parish Register, p. 49.

Isaac, a slave belonging to Robert Billups, was born on April 11, 1762. Kingston Parish Register, p. 55.

Isaac, a slave belonging to John Davis, was born on December 10, 1764. Kingston Parish Register, p. 59.

Isaac, a slave belonging to Thomas Hayes, was born on May 8, 1766. Kingston Parish Register, p. 62.

Isaac, a slave belonging to Capt. Thomas Smith, was born on June 10, 1768. Kingston Parish Register, p. 65.

Isaac, a slave belonging to James Peade, was born in April 1772 and was baptized on June 21, 1772. Kingston Parish Register, p. 69.

Isaac, a slave belonging to John Hurst, was born on July 19, 1772, and was baptized on August 16, 1772. Kingston Parish Register, p. 71.

Isaac, an adult slave belonging to John Machen, was baptized on September 13, 1772. Kingston Parish Register, p. 73.

Isaac, a slave belonging to Thomas Hewel, was born in November 1772 and was baptized on January 3, 1773. Kingston Parish Register, p. 74.

Isaac, a slave belonging to Matthias James, was born in April 1773 and was baptized on June 20, 1773. Kingston Parish Register, p. 74.

Isaac, a slave belonging to Gabriel Miller, was born on June 5, 1773, and was baptized on July 4, 1773. Kingston Parish Register, p. 75.

Isaac, a slave belonging to Joel Foster, was born in August 1774 and was baptized on August 28, 1774. Kingston Parish Register, p. 78.

Isaac, a slave belonging to George Dudley, was born in August 1774 and was baptized on October 30, 1774. Kingston Parish Register, p. 79.

Isaac, an adult slave belonging to Mann Page Esq. of Ware Parish, was baptized on May 21, 1775. Kingston Parish Register, p. 81.

Isaac, a slave belonging to Dorothy Armistead, was born in April 1776 and was baptized on June 30, 1776. Kingston Parish Register, p. 85.

Isaac, a slave belonging to John Hudgins, was born in September or October 1776 and was baptized on November 17, 1776. Kingston Parish Register, p. 86.

Isaac, a slave belonging to Robert Matthews, was born in July 1777 and was baptized on August 31, 1777. Kingston Parish Register, p. 88.

Isabell, a slave belonging to John Hayes, was born on November 15, 1753. Kingston Parish Register, p. 45.

Isabella, a slave belonging to Christopher Cully, was born on September 28, 1776, and was baptized on October 20, 1776. Kingston Parish Register, p. 86.

Ishmael, a slave belonging to Sir John Peyton, was baptized on July 28, 1772. Kingston Parish Register, p. 70.

J

Jack and Moll, twin slaves belonging to Benjamin Hodges, were born on April 14, 1750. Kingston Parish Register, p. 103.

Jack, a slave belonging to Henry Forrest, was born on August 26, 1755. Kingston Parish Register, p. 46.

Jack, a slave belonging to John Davis, was born in May 1757. Kingston Parish Register, p. 48.

Jack Barber, a slave belonging to Rose Lilly, was born on May 23, 1762. Kingston Parish Register, p. 55.

Jack, a slave belonging to Edmond Borum, was born on July 10, 1764. Kingston Parish Register, p. 59.

Jack, a slave belonging to John Lewis's estate, was born on March 20, 1769. Kingston Parish Register, p. 65.

Jack, a slave belonging to Joseph Billups, was born in October 1771 and was baptized on November 10, 1771. Kingston Parish Register, p. 68.

Jack, a slave belonging to Major William Plummer, was born in March 1772 and was baptized on May 24, 1772. Kingston Parish Register, p. 69.

Jack, a slave belonging to Jasper Clayton of Ware Parish, was born in September 1775 and was baptized on November 12, 1775. Kingston Parish Register, p. 83.

Jack, a slave belonging to Sir John Peyton, was born in late 1776 or early 1777 and was baptized on February 2, 1777. Kingston Parish Register, p. 87.

Jack, a slave belonging to Margaret Wyatt, was born in March 1777 and was baptized on May 4, 1777. Kingston Parish Register, p. 87.

Jack, an 11-year-old slave belonging to James Harris, was baptized on July 2, 1775. Kingston Parish Register, p. 82.

Jack, an adult slave belonging to Capt. John Dixon, was baptized on May 19, 1777. Kingston Parish Register, p. 87.

Jack, an adult slave belonging to Jasper Clayton of Ware Parish, was born in April 1777 and was baptized on June 15, 1777. Kingston Parish Register, p. 88.

Jackson, a slave belonging to Joseph Billups, was born on June 9, 1765. Kingston Parish Register, p. 60.

Jacob, a slave belonging to Mr. Brooks' estate, was baptized on May 13, 1750. Kingston Parish Register, p. 42.

Jacob and Esop, twin slaves belonging to Mary Plummer, were born in September 1774 and were baptized on December 4, 1774. Kingston Parish Register, p. 80.

James, a slave belonging to Mr. Brooks' estate, was baptized on April 1, 1750. Kingston Parish Register, p. 41.

James, a slave belonging to Widow Cary, was born on May 13, 1750. Kingston Parish Register, p. 41.

James, a slave belonging to Letitia Ransone, was born on September 16, 1750. Kingston Parish Register, p. 42.

James, a slave belonging to Charles Blacknall, was baptized on September 30, 1750. Kingston Parish Register, p. 42.

James, a slave belonging to Edmond Borum, was born on September 6, 1751. Kingston Parish Register, p. 43.

James, a slave belonging to John Eddins, was born on May 23, 1752. Kingston Parish Register, p. 43.

James, a slave belonging to John Billups, was born on June 17, 1753. Kingston Parish Register, p. 44.

James, a slave belonging to Capt. Gwyn Read, was born on October 15, 1754. Kingston Parish Register, p. 45.

James, a slave belonging to Richard Merchant, was born in July 1756. Kingston Parish Register, p. 47.

James, a slave belonging to John Davis, was born in November 1757. Kingston Parish Register, p. 49.

James, a slave belonging to Bristow's estate, was born on September 24, 1758. Kingston Parish Register, p. 50.

James, a slave belonging to Robert Read, was born on October 10, 1758. Kingston Parish Register, p. 50.

James, a slave belonging to Elizabeth Billups, was born on August 3, 1762. Kingston Parish Register, p. 55.

James, a slave belonging to Humphrey Billups, was born on June 1, 1763. Kingston Parish Register, p. 57.

James, a slave belonging to Richard Gwyn, was born in February 1765. Kingston Parish Register, p. 60.

James, a slave belonging to Catherine Spencer, was born on May 3, 1765. Kingston Parish Register, p. 60.

James, a slave belonging to Lucy Machen, was born in July 1765. Kingston Parish Register, p.60.

James, a slave belonging to Capt. William Hayes, was born on January 21, 1766. Kingston Parish Register, p. 61.

James, a slave belonging to Edmund Borum, was born on July 1, 1767. Kingston Parish Register, p. 63.

James, a slave belonging to Gabriel Miller, was born on July 8, 1767. Kingston Parish Register, p. 63.

James, a slave belonging to Capt. William Hayes, was born on March 20, 1768. Kingston Parish Register, p. 64.

James, a slave belonging to Elizabeth Lux, was born on December 18, 1768. Kingston Parish Register, p. 65.

James, a slave belonging to John Billups Sr., was born on July 9, 1769. Kingston Parish Register, p. 66.

James, a slave belonging to Christopher Gayle, was born on May 27, 1770. Kingston Parish Register, p. 66.

James, a slave belonging to Hugh Gwyn, was born on May 31, 1770. Kingston Parish Register, p. 66.

James, a slave belonging to Langley Billups, was born on February 10, 1771, and was baptized on March 17, 1771. Kingston Parish Register, p. 67.

James, a slave belonging to Humphrey Gwyn, was born on May 31, 1771, and was baptized on June 9, 1771. Kingston Parish Register, p. 68.

James, a slave belonging to James Davis, was born in September 1771 and was baptized on April 26, 1772. Kingston Parish Register, p. 69.

James, a small slave boy belonging to Langley Billups' estate, was born in February 1772 and was baptized on July 5, 1772. Kingston Parish Register, p. 69.

James, a slave belonging to Mary Blacknall, was born on March 3, 1772, and was baptized on April 12, 1772. Kingston Parish Register, p. 69.

James, a slave belonging to Daniel Williams, was born on April 25, 1772, and was baptized on June 21, 1772. Kingston Parish Register, p. 69.

James, a slave belonging to Sir John Peyton, was born in January 1775 and was baptized on March 23, 1775. Kingston Parish Register, p. 80.

James, a slave belonging to Sir John Peyton was born in March 1775 and was baptized on April 2, 1775. Kingston Parish Register, p. 81.

James, a slave belonging to Ann Thomas, was born on February 14, 1775, and was baptized on April 9, 1775. Kingston Parish Register, p. 81.

James, a slave belonging to John Lewis, was born in April 1775 and was baptized on May 14, 1775. Kingston Parish Register, p. 81.

James, a slave belonging to Edmund Borum Sr., was born in May 1775 and was baptized on July 2, 1775. Kingston Parish Register, p. 82.

James, an adult slave belonging to Francis Armistead's estate, was baptized on July 16, 1775. Kingston Parish Register, p. 82.

James, a slave belonging to Humphrey Gwyn, was born in September 1775 and was baptized on December 10, 1775. Kingston Parish Register, p. 83.

James, a slave belonging to John Eddins, was born in October 1775 and was baptized on December 17, 1775. Kingston Parish Register, p. 83.

James, a slave belonging to John Hurst, was born in October 1775 and was baptized on December 17, 1775. Kingston Parish Register, p. 83.

James, a slave belonging to Margaret Machen, was born in July 1776 and was baptized on July 28, 1776. Kingston Parish Register, p. 85.

James, a slave belonging to Mr. Fitzhugh, was born in March 1777 and was baptized on May 11, 1777. Kingston Parish Register, p. 87.

James, an adult slaves belonging to Digges, was baptized on July 4, 1773. Kingston Parish Register, p. 75.

James, an adult slave belonging to Ambrose Merchant, was baptized on May 21, 1775. Kingston Parish Register, p. 81.

James, Richard. See Richard James.

Jane, a slave belonging to William Hayes, was born on May 14, 1755. Kingston Parish Register, p. 46.

Jane, a slave belonging to Susanna Davis, was born in December 1756. Kingston Parish Register, p. 47.

Jane, a slave belonging to John Whiting of Ware Parish, was baptized on May 5, 1771. Kingston Parish Register, p. 70.

Jane, a slave belonging to Sir John Peyton, was baptized on November 17, 1772. Kingston Parish Register, p. 70.

Jasper, a slave boy belonging to Mrs. Ann Armistead, was born on September 11, 1750. Kingston Parish Register, p. 43.

Jasper, a slave belonging to John Eddins, was born on March 31, 1766. Kingston Parish Register, p. 61.

Jasper, a slave belonging to Robert Green, was baptized on November 3, 1772. Kingston Parish Register, p. 70.

Jasper, a slave belonging to John Eddins Sr., was born on March 7, 1775, and was baptized on April 9, 1775. Kingston Parish Register, p. 81.

Jean, a slave belonging to Thomas Hayes Jr., was born on September 19, 1753. Kingston Parish Register, p. 103.

Jemmy, a slave belonging to John Read's estate, was born on March 29, 1750. Kingston Parish Register, p.103.

Jemmy, a slave belonging to Capt. George Dudley, was baptized on April 16, 1750. Kingston Parish Register, p. 41.

Jemmy, a slave belonging to John Read of Middlesex, was baptized on May 13, 1750. Kingston Parish Register, p. 42.

Jemmy, a slave belonging to John Read of Middlesex, was baptized on May 13, 1750. Kingston Parish Register, p. 42.

Jemmy, a slave belonging to John Read's estate, was baptized on June 24, 1750. Kingston Parish Register, p. 42.

Jemmy, a slave belonging to Letitia Ransone, was baptized on September 2, 1750. Kingston Parish Register, p. 42.

Jemmy, a slave belonging to Thomas Forrest, was born in July 1756. Kingston Parish Register, p. 47.

Jemmy, a slave belonging to Harry Gwyn, was born on August 3, 1760. Kingston Parish Register, p. 53.

Jemmy, a slave belonging to John Hewel or Huel, was born on November 1, 1760. Kingston Parish Register, p. 53.

Jemmy, a slave belonging to Mathew Whiting, was born on February 27, 1763. Kingston Parish Register, p. 56.

Jemmy, a slave belonging to Joseph Billups, was born on March 29, 1763. Kingston Parish Register, p. 56.

Jemmy, a slave belonging to Capt. William Hayes, was born on July 18, 1763. Kingston Parish Register, p. 57.

Jemmy, a slave belonging to Sarah Forrest, was born on May 25, 1764. Kingston Parish Register, p. 58.

Jemmy, a slave belonging to Edward Davis, was born on September 1, 1771, and was baptized on October 13, 1771. Kingston Parish Register, p. 68.

Jemmy, a slave belonging to Robert Billups, was born on March 1, 1772, and was baptized on March 29, 1772. Kingston Parish Register, p. 69.

Jemmy, a slave belonging to Judith Minter, was born on March 18, 1772, and was baptized on April 26, 1772. Kingston Parish Register, p. 69.

Jemmy, an adult slave belonging to Robert Cully, was baptized on August 30, 1772. Kingston Parish Register, p. 72.

Jemmy, a slave belonging to Matthias James, was born in late 1772 or early 1773 and was baptized on January 31, 1773. Kingston Parish Register, p. 73.

Jemmy, a slave belonging to John Dixon Jr., was born on May 20, 1773, and was baptized on June 20, 1773. Kingston Parish Register, p. 74.

Jemmy, a slave belonging to George Brown, was born on August 12, 1774, and was baptized on September 11, 1774. Kingston Parish Register, p. 79.

Jemmy, a slave belonging to John Armistead's estate, was born on August 29, 1774, and was baptized on October 23, 1774. Kingston Parish Register, p. 79.

Jemmy, a slave belonging to William Buckner, was born in January 1775 and was baptized on March 12, 1775. Kingston Parish Register, p. 80.

Jemmy, a slave belonging to Daniel Merchant, was born in June 1775 and was baptized on July 2, 1775. Kingston Parish Register, p. 82.

Jemmy, a slave belonging to Thomas Davis, was born on February 11, 1776, and was baptized on March 24, 1776. Kingston Parish Register, p. 84.

Jemmy, a slave belonging to Samuel Williams, was born on August 11, 1777, and was baptized on October 5, 1777. Kingston Parish Register, p. 88.

Jenny, a slave girl belonging to Gwyn Read, was born in March 1750. Kingston Parish Register, p. 43.

Jenny, a slave belonging to William Callis, was born in February 1756. Kingston Parish Register, p. 47.

Jenny, a slave belonging to Ann Brooks, was born in February 1757. Kingston Parish Register, p. 48.

Jenny, a slave belonging to Richard Merchant, was born on March 1, 1757. Kingston Parish Register, p. 48.

Jenny, a slave belonging to Anthony Digges, was born on August 10, 1758. Kingston Parish Register, p. 50.

Jenny, a slave belonging to William Bond, was born on December 21, 1758. Kingston Parish Register, p. 50.

Jenny, a slave belonging to Joseph Gayle, was born in July 1759. Kingston Parish Register, p. 51.

Jenny, a slave belonging to Mary Cunningham, was born on April 11, 1760. Kingston Parish Register, p. 52.

Jenny, a slave belonging to Sheriff John Davis, was born on March 16, 1761. Kingston Parish Register, p. 54.

Jenny, a slave belonging to Ambrose Merchant, was born on March 23, 1762. Kingston Parish Register, p. 55.

Jenny, a slave belonging to Capt. John Peyton, was born on September 27, 1767. Kingston Parish Register, p. 63.

Jenny, a slave belonging to Mrs. Mary Blacknall, was born on October 10, 1767. Kingston Parish Register, p. 64.

Jenny, a slave belonging to John Respess, was born on October 25, 1767. Kingston Parish Register, p. 64.

Jenny, a slave belonging to Edmund Borum, was born on September 17, 1768. Kingston Parish Register, p. 65.

Jenny, a slave belonging to Robert Green, was born in February 1769. Kingston Parish Register, p. 65.

Jenny, a slave belonging to Joseph Billups, was born in February 1770. Kingston Parish Register, p. 66.

Jenny, a slave belonging to Joel Foster, was born on September 29, 1771, and was baptized on October 27, 1771. Kingston Parish Register, p. 68.

Jenny, an adult slave belonging to James Foster, was baptized on September 13, 1772. Kingston Parish Register, p. 73.

Jenny, a slave belonging to Mrs. Judith Plummer, was born on June 25, 1773, and was baptized on July 18, 1773. Kingston Parish Register, p. 75.

Jenny, a slave belonging to Anna Billups, was born on March 22, 1774, and was baptized on May 8, 1774. Kingston Parish Register, p. 77.

Jenny, a slave belonging to Joseph Digges, was born on May 20, 1776, and was baptized on June 30, 1776. Kingston Parish Register, p. 85.

Jenny, a slave belonging to Richard Marshant's estate, was born in July 1776 and was baptized on September 22, 1776. Kingston Parish Register, p. 86.

Jenny, a slave belonging to Matthew Gayle, was born in September or October 1776 and was baptized on November 17, 1776. Kingston Parish Register, p. 86.

Jenny, a slave belonging to Robert Billups, was born in late 1776 or early 1777 and was baptized on February 9, 1777. Kingston Parish Register, p. 87.

Jenny, a slave belonging to Major Smith, was born in March 1777 and was baptized on May 4, 1777. Kingston Parish Register, p. 87.

Jenny, a slave belonging to John Billups, was born in June 1777 and was baptized on June 29, 1777. Kingston Parish Register, p. 88.

Jenny, a slave belonging to Gabriel Hughes, was born in June 1777 and was baptized on August 24, 1777. Kingston Parish Register, p. 88.

Jenny, a slave belonging to Widow Cary of North River, was born in August 1777 and was baptized on September 17, 1777. Kingston Parish Register, p. 88.

Jenny, a slave belonging to John Billups, was born in August 1777 and was baptized on November 2, 1777. Kingston Parish Register, p. 89.

Jerry, a slave belonging to Major Kemp Plummer, was born in August 1760. Kingston Parish Register, p. 53.

Jerry, a slave belonging to Major Kemp Plummer, was born in October 1762. Kingston Parish Register, p. 56.

Jerry, a slave belonging to William Kemp, was born in March 1774 and was baptized on April 17, 1774. Kingston Parish Register, p. 7.

Jesse, a slave belonging to Robert Read, was born in February 1757. Kingston Parish Register, p. 48.

Jesse, a slave belonging to Kemp Plummer, was born on March 21, 1761. Kingston Parish Register, p. 54.

Jesse, a slave belonging to Joshua Gayle, was born on July 21, 1769. Kingston Parish Register, p. 66.

Jesse, a slave belonging to Capt. William Hayes, was born in December 1770 and was baptized on March 3, 1771. Kingston Parish Register, p. 67.

Jesse, a slave belonging to John Tabb, was born in March 1775 and was baptized on April 2, 1775. Kingston Parish Register, p. 81.

Jo, a slave belonging to John Read's estate, was born in August 1757. Kingston Parish Register, p. 48.

Jo, a slave belonging to Robert Billups, was born on June 26, 1758. Kingston Parish Register, p. 49.

Jo, a slave belonging to Francis Armistead, was born on April 8, 1763. Kingston Parish Register, p. 57.

Jo, a slave belonging to Christopher Gayle, was born on June 26, 1763. Kingston Parish Register, p. 57.

Jo, a slave belonging to Joyce Davis, was born on August 4, 1772, and was baptized on September 13, 1772. Kingston Parish Register, p. 71.

Joan, a slave belonging to Robert Spencer, was born on January 10, 1769. Kingston Parish Register, p. 65.

Joanna Joyce, a slave girl belonging to Capt. William Hayes, was born on May 8, 1762. Kingston Parish Register, p. 55.

Joe, a slave belonging to Mr. Brooks' estate, was baptized on June 3, 1750. Kingston Parish Register, p. 42.

Joe, a slave belonging to James Harper, was born in April 1773 and was baptized on July 4, 1773. Kingston Parish Register, p. 74.

Joe, a slave belonging to Hugh Gwyn, was born in June 1773 and was baptized on September 26, 1773. Kingston Parish Register, p. 76.

Joe, a slave belonging to John Armistead, was born on August 3, 1773, and was baptized on September 12, 1773. Kingston Parish Register, p. 76.

Joe, a slave belonging to William Lilly, was born in March 1776 and was baptized on June 16, 1776. Kingston Parish Register, p. 85.

Joe, a slave belonging to James Hunley, was born on March 1, 1776, and was baptized on May 5, 1776. Kingston Parish Register, p. 84.

John, a slave belonging to William Gwyn, was baptized on April 1, 1750. Kingston Parish Register, p. 41.

John, a slave belonging to John Hayes, was baptized on May 13, 1750. Kingston Parish Register, p. 41.

John, a slave belonging to William Gwyn, was baptized on June 17, 1750. Kingston Parish Register, p. 42.

John, a slave belonging to John Hayes, was baptized on September 30, 1750. Kingston Parish Register, p. 42.

John, a slave belonging to Hugh Gwyn, was born in September 1756. Kingston Parish Register, p. 47.

John, a slave belonging to Francis Degg, was born in July 1758. Kingston Parish Register, p. 50.

John, a slave belonging to Richard Merchant, was born on February 24, 1759. Kingston Parish Register, p. 50.

John, a slave belonging to Moses Hudgins, was born on January 16, 1760. Kingston Parish Register, p. 52.

John, a slave belonging to Thomas Machen's estate, was born on September 11, 1763. Kingston Parish Register, p. 57.

John, a slave belonging to Matthew Whiting, was born on October 7, 1764. Kingston Parish Register, p. 59.

John, a slave belonging to Richard Gwyn, was born on April 2, 1765. Kingston Parish Register, p. 60.

John, a slave belonging to Harry Gwyn, was born on July 15, 1765. Kingston Parish Register, p. 60.

John, a slave belonging to Capt. William Plummer, was born in February 1766. Kingston Parish Register, p. 61.

John, a slave belonging to Humphrey Billups, was born on April 28, 1766. Kingston Parish Register, p. 61.

John, a slave belonging to Humphrey Davis, was born on June 15, 1768. Kingston Parish Register, p. 65.

John, a slave belonging to Langley Billups, was born on October 8, 1768. Kingston Parish Register, p. 65.

John, a slave belonging to Elizabeth Lux, was born on January 1, 1769. Kingston Parish Register, p. 65.

John More, a slave belonging to Daniel Fitchett, was born on September 1, 1769. Kingston Parish Register, p. 66.

John Moor, a slave belonging to Matthew Whiting, was born on August 31, 1770. Kingston Parish Register, p. 66.

John Smith, a slave belonging to the Rev. John Dixon, was born on December 31, 1770, and was baptized on February 3, 1771. Kingston Parish Register, p. 67.

John, a slave belonging to the Honorable John Page of Ware Parish, was baptized on May 5, 1771. Kingston Parish Register, p. 70.

John, an adult slave belonging to Lindsey Jarvis, was baptized in 1772. Kingston Parish Register, p. 69.

John, a slave belonging to Capt. Thomas Smith, was born on February 19, 1772, and was baptized on April 12, 1772. Kingston Parish Register, p. 69.

John, a slave belonging to Henry Forrest, was born on April 6, 1772, and was baptized on June 21, 1772. Kingston Parish Register, p. 69.

John, a slave belonging to Thomas Poole, was born on July 19, 1772, and was baptized on October 25, 1772. Kingston Parish Register, p. 71.

John, an adult slave belonging to Capt. John Billups, was baptized on August 30, 1772. Kingston Parish Register, p. 72.

John, a slave belonging to Christopher Gayle's estate, was born on April 10, 1773, and was baptized on May 23, 1773. Kingston Parish Register, p. 74.

John, a slave belonging to Christopher Cully, was born on April 16, 1773, and was baptized on May 23, 1773. Kingston Parish Register, p. 74.

John, a slave boy belonging to Dawson Eddins, was baptized on July 4, 1773. Kingston Parish Register, p. 75.

John, a slave belonging to Mary Hayes, was born on October 28, 1773, and was baptized on December 5, 1773. Kingston Parish Register, p. 76.

John, a slave belonging to the Honorable John Page of Ware Parish, was born in September 1773 and was baptized on December 12, 1773. Kingston Parish Register, p. 76.

John, a slave belonging to James Hunley, a carpenter, was born in April 1773 and was baptized on February 27, 1774. Kingston Parish Register, p. 77.

John, a slave belonging to Robert Bristow's estate, was born in March 1774 and baptized on April 10, 1774. Kingston Parish Register, p. 77.

John, a slave belonging to Hugh Hayes, was born in April 1774 and was baptized on April 10, 1774. Kingston Parish Register, p. 78.

John, a slave belonging to Peter Barnet, was born in April 1774 and was baptized on July 10, 1774. Kingston Parish Register, p. 78.

John, a slave belonging to Richard Merchant's estate, was born on July 4, 1774, and was baptized on August 28, 1774. Kingston Parish Register, p. 78.

John, a slave belonging to Isaac Smith, was born on June 12, 1775, and was baptized on July 16, 1775. Kingston Parish Register, p. 82.

John, a slave belonging to Isaac Smith, was born on June 12, 1775, and was baptized on July 16, 1775. Kingston Parish Register, p. 82.

John, a slave belonging to John Armistead's estate, was born on March 9, 1776, and was baptized on May 5, 1776. Kingston Parish Register, p. 84.

John, a slave belonging to Jane Carter, was born in April 1776 and was baptized on June 23, 1776. Kingston Parish Register, p. 85.

John, a slave belonging to Josiah Foster, was born in July 1776 and was baptized on July 28, 1776. Kingston Parish Register, p. 85.

John, a slave belonging to Sir John Peyton, was born in April 1777 and was baptized on June 8, 1777. Kingston Parish Register, p. 88.

John Buck, an adult slave belonging to Philip Edward Jones, was born in April 1777 and was baptized on June 15, 1777. Kingston Parish Register, p. 88.

John, a slave belonging to William Bohannon, was born in July 1777 and was baptized on September 7, 1777. Kingston Parish Register, p. 88.

John, a slave belonging to Thomas James, was born on June 10, 1817. Kingston Parish Register, p. 90.

Johnny, an adult slave belonging to Mr. Borum, was baptized on September 25, 1774. Kingston Parish Register, p. 79.

Johnson, a slave belonging to John Cary, was baptized on May 13, 1750. Kingston Parish Register, p. 41.

Jonathan, a slave belonging to John Gayle, was born in July 1770. Kingston Parish Register, p. 66.

Jones, Betty. See Betty Jones.

Joseph, a slave belonging to Anthony Singleton, was born on February 12, 1761. Kingston Parish Register, p. 53.

Joseph, a slave belonging to Capt. Thomas Boswell of Ware Parish, was baptized on May 5, 1771. Kingston Parish Register, p. 70.

Joseph, a slave belonging to Isaac Smith, was born on April 14, 1774, and was baptized on June 19, 1774. Kingston Parish Register, p. 78.

Joseph, a slave belonging to Robert Spencer, was born in August 1774 and was baptized on October 30, 1774. Kingston Parish Register, p. 79.

Joseph, a slave belonging to James Miller, was born in late 1775 or early 1776 and was baptized on March 10, 1776. Kingston Parish Register, p. 84.

Joyce, a slave belonging to William Gwyn, was baptized on June 17, 1750. Kingston Parish Register, p. 42.

Joyce, a slave belonging to Letitia Ransone, was baptized on September 2, 1750. Kingston Parish Register, p. 42.

Joyce, a slave belonging to Richard Hunley, was baptized on September 2, 1750. Kingston Parish Register, p. 42.

Joyce, a slave belonging to William Hayes, was born on February 16, 1754. Kingston Parish Register, p. 45.

Joyce, a slave belonging to Josiah Gayle, was born on December 10, 1754. Kingston Parish Register, p. 46.

Joyce, a slave belonging to Harry Gwyn, was born on November 11, 1759. Kingston Parish Register, p. 51.

Joyce, a slave belonging to John Hayes, was born on June 5, 1760. Kingston Parish Register, p. 52.

Joyce, a slave belonging to Joseph Billups, was born on October 8, 1760. Kingston Parish Register, p. 53.

Joyce, a slave belonging to John Hunley, was born on August 26, 1762. Kingston Parish Register, p. 55.

Joyce, a slave belonging to John Hunley, was born on November 26, 1762. Kingston Parish Register, p. 56.

Joyce, a slave belonging to John Davis, was born on September 12, 1766. Kingston Parish Register, p. 62.

Joyce, a slave belonging to Ann Brooks, was born in October 1766. Kingston Parish Register, p. 62.

Joyce, a slave belonging to Robert Billups, was born on August 10, 1770. Kingston Parish Register, p. 66.

Joyce, a slave belonging to John Tompkins, was born in 1772 and was baptized on January 10, 1773. Kingston Parish Register, p. 73.

Joyce, an adult slave belonging to John Foster Jr., was baptized on September 13, 1772. Kingston Parish Register, p. 73.

Joyce, a slave belonging to John Foster, was born on August 26, 1777, and was baptized on October 5, 1777. Kingston Parish Register, p. 88.

Joyce, Joanna. See Joanna Joyce.

Joycy, an adult slave belonging to Widow Gayle, was baptized on September 13, 1772. Kingston Parish Register, p. 72.

Judah, a 5-year-old slave associated with the Kingston Parish glebe, was baptized on November 26, 1749. Kingston Parish Register, p. 41.

Judah, a slave belonging to Major Dudley, was baptized on April 16, 1750. Kingston Parish Register, p. 41.

Judah, a slave belonging to Capt. George Dudley, was baptized on April 16, 1750. Kingston Parish Register, p. 41.

Judah, a slave belonging to Richard Hunley, was baptized on May 13, 1750. Kingston Parish Register, p. 42.

Judah, a slave belonging to Mr. Brooks' estate, was baptized on May 13, 1750. Kingston Parish Register, p. 42.

Judah, a slave belonging to Mr. Ransone, was baptized on June 24, 1750. Kingston Parish Register, p. 42.

Judah, a slave belonging to William Hayes, was baptized on September 2, 1750. Kingston Parish Register, p. 42.

Judah, a slave belonging to William Hayes, was baptized on September 2, 1750. Kingston Parish Register, p. 42.

Judah, a slave belonging to Letitia Ransone, was baptized on September 16, 1750. Kingston Parish Register, p. 42.

Jude, a slave belonging to Mr. Eldris, was born on March 9, 1750. Kingston Parish Register, p. 103.

Judith, a slave girl belonging to Thomas Forrest, was born on October 14, 1752. Kingston Parish Register, p. 43.

Judith, a slave girl belonging to Anthony Digges, was born on January 3, 1753. Kingston Parish Register, p. 44.

Judith, a slave girl belonging to John Billups, was born on March 4, 1754. Kingston Parish Register, p. 45.

Judith, a slave belonging to Capt. William Hayes, was born on June 23, 1769. Kingston Parish Register, p. 65.

Judith, a slave belonging to Joseph Digges, was born on April 28, 1770. Kingston Parish Register, p. 66.

Judy, a slave belonging to Robert Bernard, was born on December 28, 1754. Kingston Parish Register, p. 46.

Judy, a slave belonging to Thomas Poole, was born in August 1757. Kingston Parish Register, p. 48.

Judy, a slave belonging to Thomas Hayes Jr., was born on September 6, 1758. Kingston Parish Register, p. 50.

Judy, a slave belonging to Anthony Digges, was born on December 26, 1762. Kingston Parish Register, p. 56.

Judy, a slave belonging to John Roots, was born in August 1763. Kingston Parish Register, p. 57.

Judy, a slave belonging to Ann Brooks, was born on June 23, 1764. Kingston Parish Register, p. 59.

Judy, a slave belonging to Mary Hayes, was born on November 25, 1765. Kingston Parish Register, p. 61.

Judy, a slave belonging to Thomas Hayes, was born on June 17, 1766. Kingston Parish Register, p. 62.

Judy, a slave belonging to Major William Plummer, was born on August 1, 1766. Kingston Parish Register, p. 62.

Judy, a slave belonging to Hugh Gwyn, was born on January 13, 1768. Kingston Parish Register, p. 64.

Judy, a slave belonging to William Armistead Esq., was born in December 1770 and was baptized on January 27, 1771. Kingston Parish Register, p. 67.

Judy, a slave belonging to Major Kemp Plummer's estate, was born on May 12, 1771, and was baptized on June 23, 1771. Kingston Parish Register, p. 68.

Judy, an adult slave belonging to Widow Gayle, was baptized on September 13, 1772. Kingston Parish Register, p. 72.

Judy, a slave belonging to John Flippin, was baptized on November 3, 1772. Kingston Parish Register, p. 70.

Judy, a slave belonging to Peter Bernard, was born in late 1772 or early 1773 and was baptized on February 7, 1773. Kingston Parish Register, p. 73.

Judy, a slave belonging to Frances Tabb, was born in July 1773 and was baptized on July 25, 1773. Kingston Parish Register, p. 75.

Judy, a slave belonging to Josiah Gayle, was born on September 19, 1773, and was baptized on October 24, 1773. Kingston Parish Register, p. 76.

Judy, a slave belonging to Joshua Gayle, was born on September 29, 1774, and was baptized on November 6, 1774. Kingston Parish Register, p. 79.

Judy, a slave belonging to Hugh Hayes, was born on February 11, 1776, and was baptized on March 24, 1776. Kingston Parish Register, p. 84.

Jugg, a slave belonging to John Jarvis, died on February 28, 1750. Kingston Parish Register, p. 103.

Juno, a slave belonging to William Elliot, was baptized on March 11, 1750. Kingston Parish Register, p. 41.

Juno, a slave belonging to Charles Blacknall, was baptized on September 30, 1750. Kingston Parish Register, p. 42.

Juno, a slave belonging to Joseph Gayle, was born on June 6, 1756. Kingston Parish Register, p. 47.

Juno, a slave belonging to John Lilly, was born on June 6, 1757. Kingston Parish Register, p. 48.

Juno, a slave belonging to Richard Merchant, was born on June 6, 1759. Kingston Parish Register, p. 51.

Juno, a slave belonging to John Respess, was born on February 3, 1761. Kingston Parish Register, p. 53.

Juno, a slave belonging to William Tompkins, was born on March 9, 1762. Kingston Parish Register, p. 55.

Juno, a slave belonging to Wilkinson Hunley, was born on May 7, 1763. Kingston Parish Register, p. 57.

Juno, a slave belonging to Mary Blacknall, was born in January 1765. Kingston Parish Register, p. 60.

Juno, a slave belonging to Christopher Gayle, was born on April 27, 1765. Kingston Parish Register, p. 60.

Juno, a slave belonging to Elizabeth Lilly, was born on October 25, 1765. Kingston Parish Register, p. 61.

Juno, a slave belonging to Christopher Cully, was born on April 3, 1768. Kingston Parish Register, p. 64.

Juno, a slave belonging to John Cary Jr., was born in June 1768. Kingston Parish Register, p. 65.

Juno, a slave belonging to William White, was born on February 16, 1769. Kingston Parish Register, p. 65.

Juno, a slave belonging to Mary Blacknall, was born on April 7, 1770. Kingston Parish Register, p. 66.

Juno, a slave belonging to John Eddins, was born on September 12, 1776, and was baptized on October 20, 1776. Kingston Parish Register, p. 66.

Juno, a female slave belonging to Gabriel Miller, was born in March 1771 and was baptized on April 14, 1771. Kingston Parish Register, p. 86.

Jupiter, a slave belonging to Mr. Ransone, was baptized on June 24, 1750. Kingston Parish Register, p. 42.

Jupiter, a slave belonging to Capt. Robert Billups, was born on November 12, 1770, and was baptized on January 6, 1771. Kingston Parish Register, p. 66.

Jupiter, a slave belonging to Capt. Robert Billups, was born on November 12, 1770, and was baptized on January 6, 1771. Kingston Parish Register, p. 67.

K

Kate, a slave belonging to John Hayes, was born on July 9, 1750. Kingston Parish Register, p. 103.

Kate, a slave belonging to Thomas Iverson's estate, was born in December 1770 and was baptized on January 27, 1771. Kingston Parish Register, p. 67.

Kate, an adult slave belonging to Francis Tabb, was baptized on August 30, 1772. Kingston Parish Register, p. 72.

Kate, an adult slave belonging to Robert Cully, was baptized on August 30, 1772. Kingston Parish Register, p. 72.

Kate, a slave belonging to Anna Billups, was born on March 12, 1773, and was baptized on May 9, 1773. Kingston Parish Register, p. 73.

Kate, an adult slave belonging to John Hudgins, was baptized on July 4, 1773. Kingston Parish Register, p. 75.

Kate, a slave belonging to Letitia Ransone, was born in May 1775 and was baptized on July 2, 1775. Kingston Parish Register, p. 82.

Katy, a slave belonging to John Armistead, was baptized on September 30, 1750. Kingston Parish Register, p. 42.

Katy, a slave belonging to Joseph Billups, was born in July 1770. Kingston Parish Register, p. 66.

Kendal, a slave belonging to George William Plummer, was born on April 14, 1773, and was baptized on May 9, 1773. Kingston Parish Register, p. 73.

Kendall, a slave belonging to George William Plummer, was born in September or October 1776 and was baptized on November 17, 1776. Kingston Parish Register, p. 86.

Kesiah, a slave belonging to William Buckner, was born in November 1776 and was baptized on January 23, 1777. Kingston Parish Register, p. 87.

Kinder or Matilder, a slave girl belonging to Capt. William Hayes, was born on September 1, 1765. Kingston Parish Register, p. 61.

Kit, a slave belonging to Richard Hunley, was baptized on September 2, 1750. Kingston Parish Register, p. 42.

Kit, a slave boy belonging to John Hayes, was born on August 28, 1752. Kingston Parish Register, p. 43.

Kit, a slave boy belonging to James Callis or Callise, was born on September 15, 1753. Kingston Parish Register, p. 44.

Kit or Kitt, a slave belonging to William Hayes, was born on October 26, 1755. Kingston Parish Register, p. 46.

Kit or Kitt, a slave belonging to John Davis, was born on July 11, 1759. Kingston Parish Register, p. 51.

Kit or Kitt, a slave belonging to John Gayle, was born on September 11, 1759. Kingston Parish Register, p. 51.

Kit, a slave belonging to Isaac Smith, was born on June 15, 1768. Kingston Parish Register, p. 65.

Kit, a slave belonging to John Foster, was born in May 1770. Kingston Parish Register, p. 66.

Kit, a slave belonging to William Armistead Esq., of Hesse, was born in November 1770 and was baptized on June 9, 1771. Kingston Parish Register, p. 67.

Kit or Kitt, a slave belonging to Peter Smith, was born on June 19, 1771, and was baptized on July 21, 1771. Kingston Parish Register, p. 68.

Kit or Kitt, a slave belonging to Mrs. Mary Davis, was baptized on July 28, 1772. Kingston Parish Register, p. 70.

Kit or Kitt, an adult slave belonging to Joseph Diggs, was baptized on September 13, 1772. Kingston Parish Register, p. 72.

Kit, a slave belonging to John Eddins, was born on September 14, 1772, and was baptized on October 25, 1772. Kingston Parish Register, p. 71.

Kit, a slave belonging to Edward Hudgins, was born on June 6, 1773, and was baptized on July 11, 1773. Kingston Parish Register, p. 75.

Kit, a slave belonging to George Forrest, was born on September 1, 1774, and was baptized on October 23, 1774. Kingston Parish Register, p. 79.

Kit, an adult slave belonging to Major Smith, was born in July 1776 and was baptized on September 8, 1776. Kingston Parish Register, p. 86.

Kit or Kitt, a slave belonging to William Stewart, was born in September or October 1776 and was baptized on November 17, 1776. Kingston Parish Register, p. 86.

Kit or Kitt, a slave belonging to Gabriel Miller, was born in July 1803. Kingston Parish Register, p. 89.

Kittenah, a slave belonging to Sir John Peyton, was born on April 28, 1773, and was baptized on June 13, 1773. Kingston Parish Register, p. 74.

Kittonah, a slave belonging to Mary Dunbar, was born on May 20, 1760. Kingston Parish Register, p. 52.

Kitty, a slave belonging to Sally Bentley, was born on March 4, 1774, and was baptized on June 5, 1774. Kingston Parish Register, p. 78.

Kitty, a slave belonging to Mary Blacknall, was born in September or October 1776 and was baptized on December 1, 1776. Kingston Parish Register, p. 86.

Kitty, a slave belonging to Joseph King, was born in February 1777 and was baptized on March 16, 1777. Kingston Parish Register, p. 87.

L

Larranie, a slave belonging to Mrs. Mary Dudley, was born in July 1759. Kingston Parish Register, p. 51.

Lawny, a slave belonging to Mildred Lilly, was born on May 2, 1762. Kingston Parish Register, p. 55.

Lena, a slave belonging to Capt. Thomas Hayes, was born in August 1772 and was baptized on September 13, 1772. Kingston Parish Register, p. 71.

Lena, a slave belonging to John Hayes, was born in February 1777 and was baptized on March 23, 1777. Kingston Parish Register, p. 87.

Leon or Lion, a slave belonging to Mr. Armistead, was baptized on April 11, 1750. Kingston Parish Register, p. 41.

Leroy, a slave belonging to Joseph Gayle, was born on December 1, 1760. Kingston Parish Register, p. 53.

Let, a slave belonging to Mrs. Cunningham, was baptized on September 30, 1750. Kingston Parish Register, p. 42.

Let or Lett, a slave belonging to John Ripley, was born on July 29, 1763. Kingston Parish Register, p. 57.

Let, a slave belonging to Mrs. Letitia Ransone, was born on June 12, 1774, and was baptized on July 17, 1774. Kingston Parish Register, p. 78.

Letitia, a slave belonging to Capt. George Dudley, was baptized on April 16, 1750. Kingston Parish Register, p. 41.

Letitia, a slave belonging to Mildred Read, was born on April 19, 1772, and was baptized on June 21, 1772. Kingston Parish Register, p. 69.

Letty, a slave belonging to Josiah Foster, was born in March 1776 and was baptized on May 19, 1776. Kingston Parish Register, p. 85.

Lewey, a slave belonging to John Davis, was born in July 1756. Kingston Parish Register, p. 47.

Lewey, a slave belonging to William Hayes, was born in December 1756. Kingston Parish Register, p. 47.

Lewey, a slave belonging to John Cary Jr., was born in December 1757. Kingston Parish Register, p. 49.

Lewey, a slave belonging to Francis Armistead, was born on April 12, 1762. Kingston Parish Register, p. 55.

Lewey, a slave belonging to William Plummer, was born on May 12, 1764. Kingston Parish Register, p. 58.

Lewey, a slave belonging to Capt. Thomas Smith, was born on February 25, 1769. Kingston Parish Register, p. 65.

Lewey, a slave belonging to Christopher Dawson, was born in February 1770. Kingston Parish Register, p. 66.

Lewey or Lewy, a slave belonging to Capt. Francis Armistead, was born on February 4, 1772, and was baptized on March 29, 1772. Kingston Parish Register, p. 69.

Lewis, a slave associated with the Kingston Parish glebe, was baptized on November 26, 1749. Kingston Parish Register, p. 41.

Lewis, a slave belonging to William Hunley, was born on September 20, 1753. Kingston Parish Register, p. 44.

Lewis, a slave belonging to Mrs. Anna Armistead, was born on April 9, 1756. Kingston Parish Register, p. 47.

Lewis, a slave belonging to John Billups, was born on January 5, 1763. Kingston Parish Register, p. 56.

Lewis, a slave belonging to Margaret Machen, was born on May 7, 1769. Kingston Parish Register, p. 65.

Lewis, a slave belonging to Richard Ransone of Ware Neck in Ware Parish, was born in December 1770 and was baptized on January 27, 1771. Kingston Parish Register, p. 67.

Lewis, a slave belonging to William Armistead Esq., was born in February 1773 and was baptized on May 2, 1773. Kingston Parish Register, p. 74.

Lewis, a slave belonging to William Armistead Esq., was born in February 1773 and was baptized on May 16, 1773. Kingston Parish Register, p. 74.

Lewis, a slave belonging to the Rev. John Dixon, was born on February 3, 1773, and was baptized on April 12, 1773. Kingston Parish Register, p. 74.

Lewis, a slave belonging to Edmund Borum, was born on June 10, 1774, and was baptized on July 17, 1774. Kingston Parish Register, p. 78.

Lewis, a slave belonging to Daniel Williams, was born on August 29, 1774, and was baptized on October 23, 1774. Kingston Parish Register, p. 79.

Lewis, a slave belonging to Jane Carter, was born in September 1774 and was baptized on December 11, 1774. Kingston Parish Register, p. 80.

Lewis, a slave belonging to Anderson Miller, was born in March 1775 and was baptized on April 2, 1775. Kingston Parish Register, p. 81.

Lewis, a slave belonging to Edward Hughes, was born on June 2, 1775, and was baptized on June 25, 1775. Kingston Parish Register, p. 81.

Lewis, a slave belonging to Mary Hayes, was born in February 1776 and was baptized on May 5, 1776. Kingston Parish Register, p. 84.

Lewis, a slave belonging to Ann Burton, was born in September 1777 and was baptized on October 19, 1777. Kingston Parish Register, p. 89.

Li or Si, a slave belonging to Richard Hunley, was baptized on September 2, 1750. Kingston Parish Register, p. 42.

Lilly, a slave belonging to Gabriel Miller, was born in March 1796. Kingston Parish Register, p. 89.

Linga, an adult slave belonging to Francis Miller, was baptized on September 13, 1772. Kingston Parish Register, p. 73.

Linus or Limus, a slave belonging to William Hayes, was baptized on September 2, 1750. Kingston Parish Register, p. 42.

Linus, a slave belonging to Major William Plummer, was born on July 8, 1773, and was baptized on August 1, 1773. Kingston Parish Register, p. 75.

Lot, a slave belonging to Richard Hunley, was baptized on May 13, 1750. Kingston Parish Register, p. 42.

Lot, a slave belonging to Richard Hunley, was baptized on May 13, 1750. Kingston Parish Register, p. 42.

Lucy, a slave girl belonging to Henry Forrest, was born on February 3, 1750. Kingston Parish Register, p. 103.

Lucy, a slave belonging to Harry Forrest, was baptized on May 13, 1750. Kingston Parish Register, p. 42.

Lucy, a slave belonging to Matthias James, was born in July 1755. Kingston Parish Register, p. 46.

Lucy, a slave belonging to George Brown, was born in September 1757. Kingston Parish Register, p. 49.

Lucy, a slave belonging to John Davis, was born in September 1757. Kingston Parish Register, p. 49.

Lucy, a slave belonging to Capt. Kemp Plummer, was born on June 11, 1758. Kingston Parish Register, p. 49.

Lucy, a slave belonging to Sarah Forrest, was born on November 6, 1758. Kingston Parish Register, p. 50.

Lucy, a slave belonging to Joseph Gayle, was born on December 18, 1758. Kingston Parish Register, p. 50.

Lucy, a slave belonging to George Hunley, was born on June 25, 1759. Kingston Parish Register, p. 51.

Lucy, a slave belonging to John Davis, was born on April 26, 1760. Kingston Parish Register, p. 52.

Lucy, a slave belonging to Capt. William Plummer, was born in September 1760. Kingston Parish Register, p. 53.

Lucy, a slave belonging to George Brown, was born in September 1760. Kingston Parish Register, p. 53.

Lucy, a slave belonging to William Gwyn, was born on June 12, 1761. Kingston Parish Register, p. 54.

Lucy, a slave belonging to John Roots, was born on September 27, 1761. Kingston Parish Register, p. 54.

Lucy, a slave belonging to Capt. William Hayes, was born on April 10, 1762. Kingston Parish Register, p. 55.

Lucy, a slave belonging to Sarah Forrest, was born on July 4, 1762. Kingston Parish Register, p. 55.

Lucy, a slave belonging to Alexander Cray, was born in November 1762. Kingston Parish Register, p. 56.

Lucy, a slave belonging to Edward Anderson, was born on March 10, 1764. Kingston Parish Register, p. 58.

Lucy, a slave belonging to Capt. William Hayes, was born on April 15, 1764. Kingston Parish Register, p. 58.

Lucy, a slave belonging to Sarah Forrest, was born on May 18, 1766. Kingston Parish Register, p. 62.

Lucy, a slave belonging to John Cary Sr., was born on February 29, 1767. Kingston Parish Register, p. 63.

Lucy, a slave belonging to Elizabeth Lewis, was born on July 24, 1767. Kingston Parish Register, p. 63.

Lucy, a slave belonging to Humphrey Gwyn, was born on April 7, 1771, and was baptized on June 23, 1771. Kingston Parish Register, p. 68.

Lucy, a slave belonging to Joseph Digges, was born in May 1771 and was baptized on June 9, 1771. Kingston Parish Register, p. 68.

Lucy, a slave belonging to Isaac Smith, was born on June 12, 1771, and was baptized on August 4, 1771. Kingston Parish Register, p. 68.

Lucy, a slave belonging to Sir John Peyton, was born in September 1772 and was baptized on November 1, 1772. Kingston Parish Register, p. 71.

Lucy, a slave belonging to Robert Cully, was born in April 1773 and was baptized on August 1, 1773. Kingston Parish Register, p. 75.

Lucy, a slave belonging to Joyce Respess, was born on August 28, 1773, and was baptized on September 26, 1773. Kingston Parish Register, p. 76.

Lucy, a slave belonging to Daniel Williams, was born in April 1774 and was baptized on July 3, 1774. Kingston Parish Register, p. 78.

Lucy, a slave belonging to John Hurst, was born on November 12, 1774, and was baptized on December 18, 1775. Kingston Parish Register, p. 80.

Lucy, a slave belonging to Capt. John Billups, was born in April 1775 and was baptized on May 7, 1775. Kingston Parish Register, p. 81.

Lucy, a slave belonging to Harry Gwyn, was born on March 25, 1775, and was baptized on May 7, 1775. Kingston Parish Register, p. 81.

Lucy, a slave belonging to Thomas Poole, was born in February 1776 and was baptized on April 14, 1776. Kingston Parish Register, p. 84.

Lucy, a slave belonging to John King, was born in April 1776 and was baptized on June 23, 1776. Kingston Parish Register, p. 85.

Lucy, a slave belonging to Humphrey Gwyn, was born in April 1776 and was baptized on June 23, 1776. Kingston Parish Register, p. 85.

Lucy, a slave belonging to Edmund Borum, was born on November 24, 1776, and was baptized on January 23, 1777. Kingston Parish Register, p. 87.

Lucy, a slave belonging to Robert Gayle, was born in late 1776 or early 1777 and was baptized on January 23, 1777. Kingston Parish Register, p. 87.

Lucy, a small slave girl belonging to William Merchant, was born in April 1777 and was baptized on June 15, 1777. Kingston Parish Register, p. 88.

Lucy, a slave belonging to Sir John Peyton, was born in July 1777 and was baptized on August 31, 1777. Kingston Parish Register, p. 88.

Lucy, a slave girl belonging to Thomas James, was born on January 25, 1795. Kingston Parish Register, p. 89.

Luke, a slave belonging to Samuel Williams, was born on May 19, 1777, and was baptized on June 29, 1777. Kingston Parish Register, p. 88.

Lydda, a slave belonging to William Lilly, was born on February 19, 1763. Kingston Parish Register, p. 56.

Lyddy, an adult slave belonging to William Hunley, was baptized on September 13, 1772. Kingston Parish Register, p. 72.

Lydia, a slave belonging to John Foster Jr., was born on May 3, 1776, and was baptized on June 30, 1776. Kingston Parish Register, p. 85.

M

Madge or Mage, a slave belonging to Capt. Thomas Smith, was born on September 24, 1764. Kingston Parish Register, p. 59.

Mahala and Cain, twin slaves belonging to Thomas James, were born on January 8, 1826. Kingston Parish Register, p. 90.

Man, a slave boy belonging to Capt. Gwyn Read, was born on June 7, 1751. Kingston Parish Register, p. 43.

Man, a slave belonging to Robert Spencer, was born in November 1772 and was baptized on January 3, 1773. Kingston Parish Register, p. 74.

Margaret, a slave belonging to George Keeble, was baptized on May 6, 1750. Kingston Parish Register, p. 41.

Margaret, a slave belonging to William Hayes, was baptized on May 13, 1750. Kingston Parish Register, p. 41.

Margaret, a slave belonging to Toy Tabb's estate, was born in February 1771 and was baptized on April 7, 1771. Kingston Parish Register, p. 67.

Margaret, a slave belonging to Gabriel Hughes, was born in March 1776 and was baptized on May 19, 1776. Kingston Parish Register, p. 85.

Margery, a slave belonging to James Ransone, was born on July 1, 1763. Kingston Parish Register, p. 57.

Marget, a slave belonging to Robert Bernard, was born on November 1, 1760. Kingston Parish Register, p. 53.

Marget, a slave belonging to Joseph Billups, was born on January 2, 1763. Kingston Parish Register, p. 56.

Marget, a slave belonging to George Dudley, was born on March 3, 1764. Kingston Parish Register, p. 58.

Maria or Murreah, a slave belonging to Christopher Dawson, was born on August 5, 1767. Kingston Parish Register, p. 63.

Martha, a slave belonging to Jane Carter, was born in February 1777 and was baptized on April 27, 1777. Kingston Parish Register, p. 87.

Mary, a slave belonging to Capt. George Dudley, was baptized on April 16, 1750. Kingston Parish Register, p. 41.

Mary, a slave belonging to Charles Jones, was baptized on June 3, 1750. Kingston Parish Register, p. 42.

Mary, a slave belonging to John Gwyn, was baptized on September 2, 1750. Kingston Parish Register, p. 42.

Mary, a slave belonging to Letitia Ransone, was baptized on September 2, 1750. Kingston Parish Register, p. 42.

Mary, a slave belonging to Letitia Ransone, was baptized on September 16, 1750. Kingston Parish Register, p. 42.

Mary, a slave child belonging to Kemp Whiting, was baptized on January 26, 1755. Kingston Parish Register, p. 87.

Mary, a slave belonging to Mrs. Anna Armistead, was born on March 25, 1756. Kingston Parish Register, p. 47.

Mary, a slave belonging to Wilkinson Hunley, was born in August 1757. Kingston Parish Register, p. 48.

Mary, a slave belonging to Robert Bernard, was born in December 1757. Kingston Parish Register, p. 49.

Mary, a slave belonging to Edward Hughes, was born on July 11, 1758. Kingston Parish Register, p. 50.

Mary, a slave belonging to Kemp Whiting, was born in September 1759. Kingston Parish Register, p. 51.

Mary, a slave belonging to Joseph Billups, was born on February 13, 1761. Kingston Parish Register, p. 53.

Mary, a slave belonging to Richard Merchant, was born in March 1761. Kingston Parish Register, p. 54.

Mary, a slave belonging to James Ransone, was born in April 1761. Kingston Parish Register, p. 54.

Mary, a slave belonging to James Ransone, was born on June 11, 1761. Kingston Parish Register, p. 54.

Mary, a slave belonging to Thomas Lewis, was born on December 7, 1761. Kingston Parish Register, p. 55.

Mary, a slave belonging to James Purcell, was born in February 1763. Kingston Parish Register, p. 56.

Mary, a slave belonging to John Respess, was born on December 27, 1763. Kingston Parish Register, p. 58.

Mary, a slave belonging to Robert Billups, was born in December 1766. Kingston Parish Register, p. 62.

Mary, a slave belonging to the Rev. John Dixon, was born on February 10, 1767. Kingston Parish Register, p. 63.

Mary, a slave belonging to John Hunley's estate, was born on March 28, 1768. Kingston Parish Register, p. 64.

Mary, a slave belonging to Harry Gwyn, was born on May 26, 1769. Kingston Parish Register, p. 65.

Mary, a slave belonging to Francis Digges, was born on July 20, 1769. Kingston Parish Register, p. 66.

Mary, a slave belonging to George Hunley, was born on November 1, 1769. Kingston Parish Register, p. 66.

Mary, a slave belonging to Langley Billups, was born in April 1770. Kingston Parish Register, p. 66.

Mary, a slave belonging to John Hudgins, was born on April 13, 1770. Kingston Parish Register, p. 66.

Mary, a slave belonging to Richard Brooks, was born on August 9, 1770. Kingston Parish Register, p. 66.

Mary, a slave belonging to Major Kemp Plummer's estate, was born on April 24, 1771, and was baptized on June 23, 1771. Kingston Parish Register, p. 68.

Mary, a slave belonging to Harry Gwyn, was born on September 6, 1771, and was baptized on October 13, 1771. Kingston Parish Register, p. 68.

Mary, a slave belonging to John Hurst, was born in October 1771 and was baptized on November 24, 1771. Kingston Parish Register, p. 68.

Mary, a slave belonging to John Billups, was born on November 24, 1771, and was baptized on December 22, 1771. Kingston Parish Register, p. 69.

Mary, a slave belonging to Joseph Billups, was born on November 28, 1771, and was baptized on December 22, 1771. Kingston Parish Register, p. 69.

Mary, a slave belonging to Isaac Smith, was born on February 22, 1772, and was baptized on July 5, 1772. Kingston Parish Register, p. 69.

Mary, a slave belonging to Hugh Hayes, was born on December 13, 1772, and was baptized on January 31, 1773. Kingston Parish Register, p. 73.

Mary, a slave belonging to Edmund Custis, was born on April 10, 1773, and was baptized on June 20, 1773. Kingston Parish Register, p. 74.

Mary, a slave belonging to Edward Anderson, was born in February 1774 and was baptized on April 10, 1774. Kingston Parish Register, p. 77.

Mary, a slave belonging to Capt. Thomas Smith, was born in March 1774 and was baptized on April 10, 1774. Kingston Parish Register, p. 77.

Mary, a slave belonging to Ambrose Merchant, was born in April 1774 and was baptized on July 3, 1774. Kingston Parish Register, p. 78.

Mary, a slave belonging to Sarah Gayle, was born on August 9, 1774, and was baptized on September 25, 1774. Kingston Parish Register, p. 79.

Mary, a slave belonging to Robert Green, was born on September 4, 1774, and was baptized on December 4, 1774. Kingston Parish Register, p. 80.

Mary, a slave belonging to Benjamin Shackelford, was born in late 1775 or early 1776 and was baptized on February 18, 1776. Kingston Parish Register, p. 84.

Mary, a slave belonging to Robert Cully, was born on February 5, 1776, and was baptized on March 24, 1776. Kingston Parish Register, p. 84.

Mary, a slave belonging to Major Thomas Smith, was born in August 1776 and was baptized on October 20, 1776. Kingston Parish Register, p. 86.

Mary, a slave belonging to Harry Gwyn, was born on April 6, 1777, and was baptized on June 1, 1777. Kingston Parish Register, p. 88.

Mary, a slave belonging to George Armistead, was born on June 27, 1777, and was baptized on July 27, 1777. Kingston Parish Register, p. 88.

Mary, a slave belonging to Thomas James, was born on March 9, 1813. Kingston Parish Register, p. 90.

Mathew, a male slave belonging to Capt. John Peyton, was born on January 14, 1753, and was baptized while he was an infant. Kingston Parish Register, p. 44.

Mathew or Matthew, a slave belonging to John Gwyn, was born on August 3, 1766. Kingston Parish Register, p. 62.

Matilda, a slave belonging to Francis Tabb, was born in March 1774 and was baptized on April 17, 1774. Kingston Parish Register, p. 77.

Matilder or Kinder, a slave girl belonging to Capt. William Hayes, was born on September 1, 1765. Kingston Parish Register, p. 61.

Matt, a slave belonging to Franky Tabb, was born in September 1772 and was baptized on November 1, 1772. Kingston Parish Register, p. 71.

Maudlin, a slave belonging to Capt. George Dudley, was baptized on April 16, 1750. Kingston Parish Register, p. 41.

Melissa, a slave belonging to Capt. George Dudley, was baptized on April 16, 1750. Kingston Parish Register, p. 41.

Mercy, a slave belonging to George Dudley Sr., was born in March 1774 and was baptized on April 17, 1774. Kingston Parish Register, p. 77.

Mildred, a slave belonging to Thomas Brooks, was baptized on April 16, 1750. Kingston Parish Register, p. 41.

Mildred, a slave belonging to John Hayes, was baptized on May 13, 1750. Kingston Parish Register, p. 41.

Mildred, a slave belonging to John Gayle, was born on March 1, 1772, and was baptized on April 12, 1772. Kingston Parish Register, p. 69.

Milly, a slave belonging to Capt. Thomas Hayes, was born on April 25, 1754. Kingston Parish Register, p. 45.

Milly, a slave belonging to Thomas Forrest, was born on August 15, 1754. Kingston Parish Register, p. 45.

Milly, a slave belonging to Robert Bernard, was born in July 1757. Kingston Parish Register, p. 48.

Milly, a slave belonging to James Davis, was born in February 1758. Kingston Parish Register, p. 49.

Milly, a slave belonging to Mordecai Cook, was born on June 26, 1758. Kingston Parish Register, p. 49.

Milly, a slave belonging to James Callis, was born on June 26, 1758. Kingston Parish Register, p. 49.

Milly, a slave belonging to Capt. William Hayes, was born on October 2, 1761. Kingston Parish Register, p. 54.

Milly, a slave belonging to Joseph Gayle, was born on October 22, 1761. Kingston Parish Register, p. 54.

Milly, a slave belonging to Mary Dunbar, was born on April 4, 1763. Kingston Parish Register, p. 57.

Milly or Milley, a slave belonging to Thomas Lewis, was born on July 27, 1763. Kingston Parish Register, p. 57.

Milly, a slave belonging to John Window, was born on January 10, 1764. Kingston Parish Register, p. 58.

Milly or Milley, a slave belonging to John Armistead, was born on January 17, 1765. Kingston Parish Register, p. 60.

Milly or Milley, a slave belonging to James Davis, was born on March 31, 1765. Kingston Parish Register, p. 60.

Milly or Milley, a slave belonging to Christopher Gayle, was born on April 27, 1765. Kingston Parish Register, p. 60.

Milly or Milley, a slave belonging to John Cary Jr., was born on January 28, 1766. Kingston Parish Register, p. 61.

Milly, a slave belonging to Capt. William Plummer, was born on March 1, 1766. Kingston Parish Register, p. 61.

Milly or Milley, a slave belonging to Thomas Hayes, was born on September 1, 1766. Kingston Parish Register, p. 62.

Milly, a slave belonging to Esther Hunley, was born on October 23, 1767. Kingston Parish Register, p. 64.

Milly, a slave belonging to Christopher Dawson, was born in April 1768. Kingston Parish Register, p. 64.

Milly, a slave belonging to John Lewis, was born on July 3, 1768. Kingston Parish Register, p. 65.

Milly, a slave belonging to Ann Brooks, was born on October 18, 1768. Kingston Parish Register, p. 65.

Milly, a slave belonging to Gabriel Miller, was born on February 22, 1769. Kingston Parish Register, p. 65.

Milly, a slave belonging to Humphrey Hudgins, was born on October 15, 1771, and was baptized on November 10, 1771. Kingston Parish Register, p. 68.

Milly, a slave belonging to James Peade, was born on April 2, 1772, and was baptized on June 21, 1772. Kingston Parish Register, p. 69

Milly, a slave belonging to Edmund Borum, was born on February 5, 1772, and was baptized on July 5, 1772. Kingston Parish Register, p. 69.

Milly, a slave belonging to John Tabb, was born in September 1772 and was baptized on November 1, 1772. Kingston Parish Register, p. 71.

Milly, a slave belonging to Richard Respess, was born in November 1772 and was baptized on June 20, 1773. Kingston Parish Register, p. 74.

Milly, a slave belonging to Francis Miller, was born on March 14, 1773, and was baptized on May 9, 1773. Kingston Parish Register, p. 73.

Milly, a slave belonging to William Armistead Esq., was born in March 1773 and was baptized on June 13, 1773. Kingston Parish Register, p. 74.

Milly, a slave belonging to George William Plummer, was born on August 12, 1773, and was baptized on September 26, 1773. Kingston Parish Register, p. 76.

Milly, a slave belonging to Gabriel Hughes, was born in 1773 and was baptized on February 6, 1774. Kingston Parish Register, p. 77.

Milly, a slave belonging to Major William Plummer, was born in April 1774 and was baptized on June 5, 1774. Kingston Parish Register, p. 78.

Milly, a slave belonging to John Callis, was born on June 25, 1774, and was baptized on July 17, 1774. Kingston Parish Register, p. 78.

Milly, a slave belonging to Robert Billups, was born on July 30, 1774, and was baptized on August 28, 1774. Kingston Parish Register, p. 78.

Milly, a slave belonging to Christopher Brown, was born on August 7, 1774, and was baptized on September 25, 1774. Kingston Parish Register, p. 79.

Milly, a slave belonging to Isaac Davis, was born on December 24, 1774, and was baptized on February 26, 1775. Kingston Parish Register, p. 80.

Milly, a slave belonging to John Digges, was born on February 16, 1776, and was baptized on May 5, 1776. Kingston Parish Register, p. 84.

Milly, a slave belonging to Tinsley or Tindsley Dixon, was born in July 1776 and was baptized on August 11, 1776. Kingston Parish Register, p. 86.

Mingo, a slave belonging to Major Kemp Plummer, was born on January 12, 1764. Kingston Parish Register, p. 58.

Mingo, a slave belonging to Gabriel Hughes, was born in November 1770 and was baptized on January 13, 1771. Kingston Parish Register, p. 67.

Minny or Minie, a slave belonging to Capt. George Dudley, was baptized on April 16, 1750. Kingston Parish Register, p. 41.

Minny, a slave belonging to Major Dudley, was baptized on April 29, 1750. Kingston Parish Register, p. 41.

Minny or Minnie, a slave belonging to Robert Read, was baptized on June 17, 1750. Kingston Parish Register, p. 42.

Minny or Minnie, a slave belonging to John Read's estate, was baptized on June 24, 1750. Kingston Parish Register, p. 42.

Minny or Minney, a slave belonging to Joseph Billups, was born in June 1757. Kingston Parish Register, p. 48.

Minny or Minney, a slave belonging to Charles Blacknall, was born on September 23, 1753. Kingston Parish Register, p. 44.

Minny or Minney, a slave belonging to George Hunley, was born on June 19, 1763. Kingston Parish Register, p. 57.

Minny or Minney, a slave belonging to Letitia Ransone, was born on April 17, 1769. Kingston Parish Register, p. 65.

Minny, a male slave belonging to Major Kemp Plummer, was born in March 1771 and was baptized on April 14, 1771. Kingston Parish Register, p. 67.

Minny, a slave belonging to Toy Tabb's estate, was baptized on November 17, 1772. Kingston Parish Register, p. 70.

Minny or Minney, a slave belonging to Peter Bernard, was born in late 1772 or early 1773 and was baptized on February 7, 1773. Kingston Parish Register, p. 73.

Minny, a slave belonging to Thomas Hewel, was born in December 1774 and was baptized on March 12, 1775. Kingston Parish Register, p. 80.

Minny, a slave belonging to Joseph King, was born in March 1775 and was baptized on April 30, 1775. Kingston Parish Register, p. 81.

Mitter, a slave girl belonging to Harry Gwyn, was born on March 23, 1761. Kingston Parish Register, p. 54.

Moll, a slave girl belonging to James Ransone, was baptized on February 9, 1749. Kingston Parish Register, p. 42.

Moll and Jack, twin slaves belonging to Benjamin Hodges, were born on April 14, 1750. Kingston Parish Register, p. 103.

Moll, a slave belonging to Elizabeth Billups, was born in November 1756. Kingston Parish Register, p. 47.

Moll, a slave belonging to Major Kemp Plummer, was born on August 12, 1765. Kingston Parish Register, p. 60.

Molly, a slave belonging to George Keeble, was born on January 23, 1750. Kingston Parish Register, p. 43.

Molly, a slave belonging to Robert Read, was baptized on April 29, 1750. Kingston Parish Register, p. 41.

Molly, a slave belonging to Major Dudley, was baptized on April 29, 1750. Kingston Parish Register, p. 41.

Molly, a slave belonging to Mr. Ransone, was baptized on June 24, 1750. Kingston Parish Register, p. 42.

Molly, a slave belonging to George Keeble, was baptized in May 1751. Kingston Parish Register, p. 179.

Molly, a slave belonging to Anthony Singleton, was born on May 14, 1763. Kingston Parish Register, p. 57.

Molly, a slave belonging to George Brooks, was born on September 22, 1771, and was baptized on October 27, 1771. Kingston Parish Register, p. 68.

Molly, a slave belonging to John Foster Sr., was born on October 20, 1771, and was baptized on November 24, 1771. Kingston Parish Register, p. 69.

Molly, an adult slave belonging to Gabriel Miller, was baptized on September 13, 1772. Kingston Parish Register, p. 72.

Molly, a slave belonging to Dorothy Cary, was born in October 1772 and was baptized on December 13, 1772. Kingston Parish Register, p. 71.

Molly, a slave belonging to John Page Esq. of Ware Parish, was born in February 1773 and was baptized on April 4, 1773. Kingston Parish Register, p. 73.

Molly, an adult slave belonging to James Davis, was baptized on July 4, 1773. Kingston Parish Register, p. 75.

Molly, a slave belonging to Ann Cary, was born in August 1774 and was baptized on September 18, 1774. Kingston Parish Register, p. 79.

Molly, a slave belonging to William Morris's estate, was born in May 1776 and was baptized on July 14, 1776. Kingston Parish Register, p. 85.

Molly, a slave belonging to Sir John Peyton, was born in July 1777 and was baptized on August 31, 1777. Kingston Parish Register, p. 88.

Moor, John. See John Moor.

More, John. See John More.

Moro, a slave girl belonging to Joshua Foster, was born in March 1774 and was baptized on May 8, 1774. Kingston Parish Register, p. 77.

Morris, a slave belonging to Mrs. Lux, was baptized on June 16, 1772. Kingston Parish Register, p. 70.

Moses, a slave belonging to John Hayes, was baptized on April 22, 1750. Kingston Parish Register, p. 41.

Moses, a slave belonging to Major William Plummer, was born in May 1771 and was baptized on May 24, 1772. Kingston Parish Register, p. 69.

Moses, a slave belonging to Mann Page Esq. of Ware Parish, was born in December 1774 and was baptized on February 5, 1775. Kingston Parish Register, p. 80.

N

Nan, a slave belonging to John Davis, was born on November 15, 1754. Kingston Parish Register, p. 45.

Nan, a slave belonging to James Davis, was born on May 1, 1757. Kingston Parish Register, p. 48.

Nan, a slave belonging to James Ransone, was born on May 2, 1765. Kingston Parish Register, p. 60.

Nan, a slave belonging to Mrs. Lux, was baptized on May 5, 1771. Kingston Parish Register, p. 70.

Nancy, a slave belonging to John Read of Middlesex, was baptized on May 13, 1750. Kingston Parish Register, p. 42.

Nancy, a slave belonging to John Hudgins, was born on October 24, 1773, and was baptized on December 5, 1773. Kingston Parish Register, p. 76.

Nancy, a slave belonging to Major Thomas Smith, was born on August 20, 1774, and was baptized on September 11, 1774. Kingston Parish Register, p. 79.

Nancy, a slave belonging to Francis Tabb, was born in August 1774 and was baptized on October 30, 1774. Kingston Parish Register, p. 79.

Nancy, a slave belonging to George Alexander Dudley, was born in October or November 1774 and was baptized on January 8, 1775. Kingston Parish Register, p. 80.

Nancy, a slave belonging to Frances Tabb, was born in May 1775 and was baptized on July 9, 1775. Kingston Parish Register, p. 82.

Nancy, a slave child belonging to Isaac Foster, was baptized on July 16, 1775. Kingston Parish Register, p. 82.

Nancy, a slave belonging to Dorothy Cary, was born in April 1776 and was baptized on June 23, 1776. Kingston Parish Register, p. 85.

Nancy, a slave belonging to Henry Forrest, was born in September 1776 and was baptized on October 20, 1776. Kingston Parish Register, p. 86.

Nancy, a slave belonging to Major Thomas Smith, was born in November 1776 and was baptized on January 23, 1777. Kingston Parish Register, p. 87.

Nanny, a slave belonging to Robert Read, was baptized on April 29, 1750. Kingston Parish Register, p. 41.

Nanny, a slave belonging to William Hayes, was baptized on September 2, 1750. Kingston Parish Register, p. 42.

Nanny, a slave belonging to Capt. Read, was baptized on September 16, 1750. Kingston Parish Register, p. 42.

Nanny, a slave belonging to Robert Read, was born on May 23, 1754. Kingston Parish Register, p. 45.

Nanny, a slave belonging to Thomas Poole, was born in December 1755. Kingston Parish Register, p. 46.

Nanny, a slave belonging to Thomas Poole, was born in May 1756. Kingston Parish Register, p. 47.

Nanny, a slave belonging to Harry Gwyn, was born on October 14, 1756. Kingston Parish Register, p. 47.

Nanny, a slave belonging to John Lilly, was born in December 1756. Kingston Parish Register, p. 47.

Nanny, a slave belonging to William Hayes, was born on March 19, 1759. Kingston Parish Register, p. 50.

Nanny, a slave belonging to John Davis Sr., was born in July 1759. Kingston Parish Register, p. 51.

Nanny, a slave belonging to Thomas Hayes Jr., was born on April 7, 1760. Kingston Parish Register, p. 52.

Nanny, a slave belonging to John Foster, was born on December 29, 1762. Kingston Parish Register, p. 56.

Nanny, a slave belonging to Harry Gwyn, was born on January 25, 1763. Kingston Parish Register, p. 56.

Nanny, a slave belonging to Dorothy Read, was born in September 1763. Kingston Parish Register, p. 57.

Nanny, a slave belonging to Joseph Digges, was born on April 15, 1764. Kingston Parish Register, p. 58.

Nanny, a slave belonging to James Purcell, was born on October 6, 1764. Kingston Parish Register, p. 59.

Nanny, a slave belonging to Francis Armistead, was born on April 11, 1765. Kingston Parish Register, p. 60.

Nanny, a slave belonging to Robert Foster, was born on July 28, 1765. Kingston Parish Register, p. 60.

Nanny, a slave belonging to John Billups, was born in February 1766. Kingston Parish Register, p. 61.

Nanny, a slave belonging to John Respess, was born in February 1766. Kingston Parish Register, p. 61.

Nanny, a slave belonging to Capt. William Hayes, was born on April 30, 1766. Kingston Parish Register, p. 61.

Nanny, a slave belonging to Capt. William Hayes, was born on June 25, 1766. Kingston Parish Register, p. 62.

Nanny, a slave belonging to George Dudley, was born in November 1766. Kingston Parish Register, p. 62.

Nanny, a slave belonging to George Hunley, was born in November 1767. Kingston Parish Register, p. 64.

Nanny, a slave belonging to the Rev. John Dixon, was born on December 11, 1768. Kingston Parish Register, p. 65.

Nanny, a slave belonging to Isaac Foster, was born in July 1775 and was baptized on July 16, 1775. Kingston Parish Register, p. 83.

Nanny, a slave belonging to Sir John Peyton, was born in September or October 1776 and was baptized on December 15, 1776. Kingston Parish Register, p. 86.

Nat, a slave belonging to Mr. Brooks, was baptized on June 24, 1750. Kingston Parish Register, p. 42.

Nat, a slave belonging to John Gwyn, was born on November 10, 1753. Kingston Parish Register, p. 45.

Nat, a slave belonging to Capt. Robert Billups, was born in January 1770. Kingston Parish Register, p. 66.

Nat, a slave belonging to Charles Jones, as born in February 1773 and was baptized on May 2, 1773. Kingston Parish Register, p. 74.

Nat, a slave belonging to John Hayes, was born in July 1776 and was baptized on August 25, 1776. Kingston Parish Register, p. 86.

Nathaniel, a slave belonging to Edmund Custis, was born on October 18, 1774, and was baptized on December 18, 1775. Kingston Parish Register, p. 80.

Neaton, a slave belonging to William Gwyn, was baptized on June 17, 1750. Kingston Parish Register, p. 42.

Neaton, a slave girl belonging to Charles Blacknall, was born on January 10, 1761. Kingston Parish Register, p. 53.

Ned, a slave belonging to Anthony Digges Jr., was born on May 13, 1754. Kingston Parish Register, p. 45.

Ned, a slave belonging to Anna Billups, was born in September 1771 and was baptized on October 27, 1771. Kingston Parish Register, p. 68.

Ned, a slave belonging to Edward Matthews, was born in May 1775 and was baptized on July 9, 1775. Kingston Parish Register, p. 82.

Nell, a slave belonging to Benjamin Hodges, was born on May 7, 1750. Kingston Parish Register, p. 103.

Nell, a slave belonging to John Read's estate, was baptized on June 24, 1750. Kingston Parish Register, p. 42.

Nell, a slave girl belonging to Capt. Gwyn Read, was born on December 19, 1752. Kingston Parish Register, p. 43.

Nell, a slave belonging to Mordecai Cook, was born in May 1756. Kingston Parish Register, p. 47.

Nell, a slave belonging to James Hodges, was born on May 7, 1757. Kingston Parish Register, p. 48.

Nell, a slave belonging to Robert Billups, was born in July 1759. Kingston Parish Register, p. 51.

Nell, a slave belonging to Humphrey Billups, was born on December 15, 1760. Kingston Parish Register, p. 53.

Nell, a slave belonging to James Ransone, was born on February 25, 1761. Kingston Parish Register, p. 53.

Nell, an adult slave belonging to Isaac Smith, was baptized on July 16, 1775. Kingston Parish Register, p. 82.

Nell, a slave belonging to William Armistead Esq., was born in September 1775 and was baptized on December 10, 1775. Kingston Parish Register, p. 83.

Nell, a slave belonging to Dorothy Cary, was born in August 1777 and was baptized on October 26, 1777. Kingston Parish Register, p. 89.

Nelson, a slave belonging to Letitia Ransone, was born on September 29, 1771, and was baptized on November 10, 1771. Kingston Parish Register, p. 68.

Nelson, a slave belonging to Sir John Peyton, was baptized on July 28, 1772. Kingston Parish Register, p. 70.

Nelson, a slave belonging to Currel Armistead, was born on August 5, 1773, and was baptized on September 26, 1773. Kingston Parish Register, p. 76.

Nelson, a slave belonging to Humphrey Gwyn, was born on February 21, 1775, and was baptized on April 9, 1775. Kingston Parish Register, p. 81.

Nelson, a slave belonging to John Hayes, was born on July 18, 1777, and was baptized on August 24, 1777. Kingston Parish Register, p. 88.

Nelson, a slave belonging to John Lewis, was born on August 4, 1777, and was baptized on September 7, 1777. Kingston Parish Register, p. 88.

Nelson, a slave belonging to Thomas James, was born on September 20, 1800. Kingston Parish Register, p. 89.

Nero, a slave belonging to Richard Hunley, was baptized on September 2, 1750. Kingston Parish Register, p. 42.

Nero, a slave belonging to Capt. Thomas Machen, was born in July 1756. Kingston Parish Register, p. 47.

Nero, a slave belonging to Sir John Peyton, was born in July 1776 and was baptized on August 4, 1776. Kingston Parish Register, p. 86.

Netty, a slave belonging to Sarah Forrest, was baptized on June 10, 1750. Kingston Parish Register, p. 42.

Nulty, a slave belonging to John Eddins, was born on July 26, 1768. Kingston Parish Register, p. 65.

O

Oliver, a slave belonging to John Cary's estate, was born in March 1769. Kingston Parish Register, p. 65.

Oliver, a slave belonging to Sir John Peyton, was born in February 1776 and was baptized on April 28, 1776. Kingston Parish Register, p. 84.

Oliver, a slave belonging to Robert Billups, was born in September or October 1776 and was baptized on December 1, 1776. Kingston Parish Register, p. 86.

P

Page, a slave belonging to Anna Armistead, was born on September 24, 1756. Kingston Parish Register, p. 47.

Page, a slave belonging to Edmund Borum, was born on June 20, 1759. Kingston Parish Register, p. 51.

Page, a slave belonging to George Brown, was born on September 4, 1765. Kingston Parish Register, p. 61.

Page, an adult female slave belonging to Robert Cully, was baptized on August 20, 1772. Kingston Parish Register, p. 72.

Page, a slave belonging to John Elliott, was baptized on November 3, 1772. Kingston Parish Register, p. 70.

Page, an adult slave belonging to Mr. Borum, was baptized on September 25, 1774. Kingston Parish Register, p. 79.

Page, a slave girl belonging to John Armistead's estate, was born on May 20, 1777, and was baptized on June 29, 1777. Kingston Parish Register, p. 88.

Pagy, a slave girl whose owner's name was not listed in the parish register, was baptized on January 4, 1778. Kingston Parish Register, p. 89.

Pamelia, a slave belonging to John Gwyn, was born on November 7, 1755. Kingston Parish Register, p. 46.

Parker, a slave belonging to Miss Rosanna Lilly, was born on January 1, 1774, and was baptized on February 13, 1774. Kingston Parish Register, p. 77.

Parker, Daniel. See Daniel Parker.

Pat or Patt, a slave belonging to the Rev. John Dixon, was born on October 19, 1753. Kingston Parish Register, p. 44.

Pat, a slave belonging to the Rev. John Dixon, was born on March 8, 1760. Kingston Parish Register, p. 52.

Pat or Patt, a slave belonging to Capt. John Clayton of Ware Parish, was born in March 1771 and was baptized on April 21, 1771. Kingston Parish Register P. 67.

Pat or Patt, a slave belonging to John Clayton of Ware Parish, was baptized on April 21, 1771. Kingston Parish Register p. 70.

Pat, a slave belonging to Isaac Smith, was born on June 15, 1772, and was baptized on August 2, 1772. Kingston Parish Register, p. 71.

Patience, a slave belonging to Catherine Spencer, was born on May 4, 1762. Kingston Parish Register, p. 55.

Patience, a slave belonging to Thomas Hayes, was born on February 20, 1763. Kingston Parish Register, p. 56.

Patience, a slave belonging to Capt. Thomas Hayes, was born on April 29, 1773, and was baptized on July 4, 1773. Kingston Parish Register, p. 74.

Patience, a slave belonging to John Carter, was born in March 1774 and was baptized on April 17, 1774. Kingston Parish Register, p. 77.

Patty, a slave girl belonging to Gwyn Read, was born on March 5, 1750. Kingston Parish Register, p. 103.

Patty, a slave girl belonging to Anna or Ann Armistead, was born on March 26, 1752. Kingston Parish Register, p. 43.

Patty, a slave belonging to Hugh Gwyn, was born in September 1756. Kingston Parish Register, p. 47.

Patty, a slave belonging to Thomas Brooks, was born on January 8, 1763. Kingston Parish Register, p. 56.

Patty, a slave belonging to John Eddins, was born on June 4, 1764. Kingston Parish Register, p. 59.

Patty, a slave belonging to John Gayle, was born in June 1768. Kingston Parish Register, p. 65.

Patty, a slave belonging to Mrs. Mary Blacknall, was born on December 13, 1770, and was baptized on January 20, 1771. Kingston Parish Register, p. 67.

Patty, a slave belonging to Walter Keeble, was born on September 13, 1772, and was baptized on October 25, 1772. Kingston Parish Register, p. 71.

Patty, a slave belonging to Harry Gwyn, was born on April 7, 1773, and was baptized on May 9, 1773. Kingston Parish Register, p. 73.

Patty, a slave belonging to Frances Tabb, was born on July 1, 1773, and was baptized on July 25, 1773. Kingston Parish Register, p. 75.

Patty, a slave belonging to John Armistead, was born on December 6, 1773, and was baptized on March 13, 1774. Kingston Parish Register, p. 77.

Patty, a slave belonging to Rosanna Lilly, was born in February 1774 and was baptized on April 10, 1774. Kingston Parish Register, p. 77.

Patty, a slave belonging to William Armistead Esq., was born in April 1774 and was baptized on June 12, 1774. Kingston Parish Register, p. 78.

Patty, a slave belonging to Sir John Peyton, was born in late 1775 or early 1776 and was baptized on February 18, 1776. Kingston Parish Register, p. 84.

Patty, a slave belonging to James Carter, was born in August 1777 and was baptized on October 26, 1777. Kingston Parish Register, p. 89.

Peg, a slave belonging to Henry Forrest, was baptized on June 24, 1750. Kingston Parish Register, p. 42.

Peg, a slave belonging to Langley Billups, was born on October 8, 1750. Kingston Parish Register, p. 43.

Peg, a slave belonging to James Ransone, was born on June 22, 1759. Kingston Parish Register, p. 51.

Peg, a slave belonging to John Gwyn, was born on June 14, 1760. Kingston Parish Register, p. 52.

Peg, a slave belonging to Thomas Hayes Jr., was born on October 9, 1760. Kingston Parish Register, p. 53.

Peg, a slave belonging to Capt. Thomas Smith, was born on January 18, 1766. Kingston Parish Register, p. 61.

Peg, a slave belonging to Capt. Francis Armistead, was born on April 8, 1767. Kingston Parish Register, p. 63.

Peg, a slave belonging to John Davis, was born on July 4, 1767. Kingston Parish Register, p. 63.

Peg, a slave belonging to Humphrey Billups, was born in March 1768. Kingston Parish Register, p. 64.

Peg, a slave belonging to Major Kemp Plummer, was born on September 3, 1768. Kingston Parish Register, p. 65.

Peg, an adult slave belonging to Robert Cully, was baptized on August 30, 1772. Kingston Parish Register, p. 72.

Peg, a slave belonging to Dorothy Matthews, was born in April 1774 and was baptized on May 15, 1774. Kingston Parish Register, p. 78.

Peg, a slave belonging to Peter Bernard, was born on August 24, 1777, and was baptized on October 19, 1777. Kingston Parish Register, p. 89.

Peggy, a slave belonging to William Armistead Esq., was born in September 1775 and was baptized on December 1, 1775. Kingston Parish Register, p. 83.

Pendar, a slave belonging to Robert Read, was born in November 1760. Kingston Parish Register, p. 53.

Peter, a slave belonging to William Gwyn, was born on February 21, 1750. Kingston Parish Register, p. 43.

Peter, a slave belonging to Major Dudley, was baptized on April 16, 1750. Kingston Parish Register, p. 41.

Peter, a slave belonging to Thomas Brooks, was baptized on April 16, 1750. Kingston Parish Register, p. 41.

Peter, a slave belonging to Capt. George Dudley, was baptized on April 16, 1750. Kingston Parish Register, p. 41.

Peter, a slave belonging to Hugh Gwyn, was baptized on April 29, 1750. Kingston Parish Register, p. 41.

Peter, a slave belonging to Thomas Poole, was baptized on May 6, 1750. Kingston Parish Register, p. 41.

Peter, a slave belonging to William Tabb, was baptized on September 9, 1750. Kingston Parish Register, p. 42.

Peter, a slave belonging to Charles Blacknall, was baptized on September 30, 1750. Kingston Parish Register, p. 42.

Peter, a slave belonging to Banister Jarvis, died on January 29, 1752. Kingston Parish Register, p. 179.

Peter, a slave belonging to Thomas Forrest, was born on July 13, 1752. Kingston Parish Register, p. 43.

Peter, a slave belonging to James Callis Sr., was born on October 1, 1752. Kingston Parish Register, p. 43.

Peter, a slave belonging to James Hayes, was born on June 4, 1753. Kingston Parish Register, p. 44,

Peter, a slave belonging to Matthias James, was born in November 1757. Kingston Parish Register, p. 49.

Peter, a slave belonging to John Callis, was born on December 19, 1757. Kingston Parish Register, p. 49.

Peter, a slave belonging to the Rev. John Dixon, was born on December 14, 1758. Kingston Parish Register, p. 50.

Peter, a slave belonging to John Billups, was born on May 20, 1759. Kingston Parish Register, p. 51.

Peter, a slave belonging to John Machen or Michen, was born in November 1759. Kingston Parish Register, p. 51.

Peter, a slave belonging to Alexander Cray, was born on March 10, 1760. Kingston Parish Register, p. 52.

Peter, a slave belonging to John Edden, was born on October 2, 1761. Kingston Parish Register, p. 54.

Peter, a slave belonging to James Purcell, was born in January 1763. Kingston Parish Register, p. 56.

Peter, a slave belonging to Isaac Smith, was born on July 2, 1763. Kingston Parish Register, p. 57.

Peter, a slave belonging to Capt. William Plummer, was born in September 1763. Kingston Parish Register, p. 57.

Peter, a slave belonging to Bristow's estate, was born on May 1, 1764. Kingston Parish Register, p. 58.

Peter, a slave belonging to Francis Digges, was born on January 31, 1765. Kingston Parish Register, p. 60.

Peter, a slave belonging to John Armistead, was born on August 14, 1767. Kingston Parish Register, p. 63.

Peter, a slave belonging to Major Kemp Plummer, was born on October 11, 1767. Kingston Parish Register, p. 64.

Peter, a slave belonging to Gabriel Miller, was born on June 27, 1768. Kingston Parish Register, p. 65.

Peter, a slave belonging to Edward Anderson, was born in August 1768. Kingston Parish Register, p. 65.

Peter, a slave belonging to Letitia Ransone, was born on December 20, 1768. Kingston Parish Register, p. 65.

Peter, a slave belonging to Major Kemp Plummer, was born on January 8, 1769. Kingston Parish Register, p. 65.

Peter, a slave belonging to George Forrest, was born on February 5, 1769. Kingston Parish Register, p. 65.

Peter, a slave belonging to Capt. Thomas Smith, was born on April 6, 1769. Kingston Parish Register, p. 65.

Peter, a slave belonging to Capt. Francis Armistead, was born on May 31, 1769. Kingston Parish Register, p. 65.

Peter, a slave belonging to Ambrose Merchant, was born in June 1769. Kingston Parish Register, p. 65.

Peter, a slave belonging to Ambrose Merchant, was born in July 1770. Kingston Parish Register, p. 66.

Peter, a slave belonging to William Callis, was born on December 24, 1770, and was baptized on February 3, 1771. Kingston Parish Register, p. 67,

Peter, a slave belonging to George Dudley, was baptized on May 5, 1771. Kingston Parish Register, p. 70.

Peter, an adult slave belonging to Robert Cully, was baptized on August 30, 1772. Kingston Parish Register, p. 72.

Peter, an adult slave belonging to William Lilly, was baptized on August 30, 1772. Kingston Parish Register, p. 72.

Peter, an adult slave belonging to Joseph Billups, was baptized on September 13, 1772. Kingston Parish Register, p. 72.

Peter, an adult slave belonging to Humphrey Hudgins, was baptized on September 13, 1772. Kingston Parish Register, p. 72.

Peter, an adult slave belonging to Thomas Billups, was baptized on July 4, 1773. Kingston Parish Register, p. 75.

Peter, a slave belonging to Sir John Peyton, was born in February 1773 and was baptized on April 4, 1773. Kingston Parish Register, p. 73.

Peter, a slave belonging to James Davis, was born on January 10, 1773, and was baptized on May 9, 1773. Kingston Parish Register, p. 73.

Peter, a slave belonging to Robert Billups, was born in April 1773 and was baptized on May 23, 1773. Kingston Parish Register, p. 74.

Peter, a slave belonging to Josiah Harris, was born on July 22, 1773, and was baptized on September 12, 1773. Kingston Parish Register, p. 76.

Peter, a slave belonging to John Gayle, was born in February 1774 and was baptized on June 5, 1774. Kingston Parish Register, p. 78.

Peter, a slave belonging to Andrew Kerr, was born on August 27, 1774, and was baptized on September 25, 1774. Kingston Parish Register, p. 79.

Peter, a slave belonging to James Parsons, was born in December 1774 and was baptized on January 15, 1775. Kingston Parish Register, p. 80.

Peter, a slave belonging to Holder Hudgins, was born in June 1775 and was baptized on August 27, 1775. Kingston Parish Register, p. 83.

Peter, a slave belonging to John Foster, was born in July 1775 and was baptized on July 16, 1775. Kingston Parish Register, p. 83.

Peter, a slave child belonging to John Foster, was baptized on July 16, 1775. Kingston Parish Register, p. 82.

Peter, a slave belonging to Charles Debnam, was born in late 1775 or early 1776 and was baptized on January 21, 1776. Kingston Parish Register, p. 84.

Peter, a slave belonging to Thomas Hayes, was born on February 14, 1776, and was baptized on March 24, 1776. Kingston Parish Register, p. 84.

Peter, a slave belonging to George Armistead, was born on September 1, 1776, and was baptized on October 20, 1776. Kingston Parish Register, p. 86.

Peyton Collier, a slave belonging to Thomas James, was born on September 7, 1822. Kingston Parish Register, p. 90.

Phebe, a slave belonging to Capt. George Dudley, was baptized on April 16, 1750. Kingston Parish Register, p. 41.

Phebe, a slave belonging to William Hayes, was born on December 11, 1759. Kingston Parish Register, p. 51.

Phebe, a slave belonging to Jasper Clayton of Ware Parish, was baptized on May 5, 1771. Kingston Parish Register, p. 70.

Phebe, a slave belonging to Daniel Williams, was born in January 1775 and was baptized on March 12, 1775. Kingston Parish Register, p. 80.

Phil, a slave belonging to John Armistead, was baptized on September 9, 1750. Kingston Parish Register, p. 42.

Phil, a slave boy belonging to Gwyn Read, was born on October 25, 1752. Kingston Parish Register, p. 43.

Phil, a slave belonging to Capt. Thomas Machen, was born in July 1756. Kingston Parish Register, p. 47.

Phil or Phill, a slave belonging to Mrs. Anna Armistead, was born on October 1, 1756. Kingston Parish Register, p. 47.

Phil, a slave belonging to Isaac Davis, was born on June 10, 1762. Kingston Parish Register, p. 55.

Phil or Phill, a slave belonging to Gabriel Miller, was born on July 3, 1765. Kingston Parish Register, p. 60.

Phil or Phill, a slave belonging to William Tompkins, was born on April 21, 1766. Kingston Parish Register, p. 61.

Phil, a slave belonging to Major William Plummer, was born in December 1767. Kingston Parish Register, p. 64.

Phil, a slave belonging to Henry Forrest, was born on September 10, 1769. Kingston Parish Register, p. 66.

Phil, a slave belonging to John Elliott Jr., was born in March 1771 and was baptized on April 3, 1771. Kingston Parish Register, p. 67.

Phil or Phill, a slave belonging to John Elliott Jr., was baptized on April 21, 1771. Kingston Parish Register, p. 70.

Phil or Phill, a slave belonging to Thomas Iverson's estate, was baptized on May 5, 1771. Kingston Parish Register, p. 70.

Phil or Phill, a slave belonging to Humphrey Billups, was born on August 30, 1772, and was baptized on October 25, 1772. Kingston Parish Register, p. 71.

Phil, a slave belonging to Joyce Gayle, was born on October 25, 1774, and was baptized on December 4, 1774. Kingston Parish Register, p. 80.

Phil or Phill, a slave belonging to Hugh Gwyn, was born in March 1775 and was baptized on April 2, 1775. Kingston Parish Register, p. 81.

Phil or Phill, a slave belonging to Sir John Peyton, was born in August 1775 and was baptized on October 1, 1775. Kingston Parish Register, p. 83.

Phil, a slave belonging to Sir John Peyton, was born in late 1775 or early 1776, and was baptized on February 18, 1776. Kingston Parish Register, p. 84.

Phil, a slave belonging to William Elliott, was born in late 1775 or early 1776 and was baptized on March 3, 1776. Kingston Parish Register, p. 84.

Phil, a slave belonging to Edward Tabb, was born in February 1776 and was baptized on May 5, 1776. Kingston Parish Register, p. 84.

Phil, a slave belonging to Joseph Digges, was born in August 1777 and was baptized on November 2, 1777. Kingston Parish Register, p. 89.

Philibery, a slave belonging to William Tabb, was baptized on July 1, 1750. Kingston Parish Register, p. 42.

Philip or Phillip, a slave belonging to John Peyton, was born on April 27, 1759. Kingston Parish Register, p. 51.

Philip, a slave belonging to Francis Digges, was born in October 1760. Kingston Parish Register, p. 53.

Philip, a slave belonging to Major Kemp Plummer, was born in July 1762. Kingston Parish Register, p. 55.

Philip, a slave belonging to George Brown, was born in January 1764. Kingston Parish Register, p. 58.

Philip, a slave belonging to William Callis, was born on August 21, 1764. Kingston Parish Register, p. 59.

Philip, a slave belonging to Augustine Curtis, was born in March 1771 and was baptized on April 21, 1771. Kingston Parish Register, p. 67.

Phillis, a slave belonging to William Elliott, was baptized on March 11, 1750. Kingston Parish Register, p. 41.

Phillis, a slave belonging to Captain George Dudley, was baptized on April 16, 1750. Kingston Parish Register, p. 41.

Phillis, a slave belonging to Capt. Plummer, was baptized on April 29, 1750. Kingston Parish Register, p. 41.

Phillis, a slave belonging to John Read of Middlesex County, was baptized on May 13, 1750. Kingston Parish Register, p. 42.

Phillis, a slave belonging to Letitia Ransone, was baptized on September 30, 1750. Kingston Parish Register, p. 42.

Phillis or Philas, a slave belonging to Dorothy Brooks, was born in February 1762. Kingston Parish Register, p. 55.

Phillis, a slave belonging to George Forrest, was born on March 9, 1764. Kingston Parish Register, p. 58.

Phillis or Philis, a slave belonging to Major Kemp Plummer, was born in February 1768. Kingston Parish Register, p. 64.

Phillis or Philis, a slave belonging to Joseph Digges, was born on December 4, 1768. Kingston Parish Register, p. 65.

Phillis or Philis, a slave belonging to John Respess, was born on June 27, 1769. Kingston Parish Register, p. 65.

Phillis, a slave belonging to Kemp Plummer's estate, was born in February 1771 and was baptized on June 9, 1771. Kingston Parish Register, p. 67.

Phillis, a slave belonging to Augustine Curtis, was baptized on April 21, 1771. Kingston Parish Register, p. 70.

Phillis, a slave belonging to William Lilly, was born on October 3, 1771, and was baptized on November 10, 1771. Kingston Parish Register, p. 68.

Phillis, a slave belonging to John Dixon Jr., was born in late 1772 or early 1773 and was baptized on February 14, 1773. Kingston Parish Register, p. 76.

Phillis, a slave belonging to John Foster Jr., was born on August 2, 1773, and was baptized on September 26, 1773. Kingston Parish Register, p. 76.

Phillis, an adult slave of William Merchant, was baptized on August 30, 1772. Kingston Parish Register, p. 72.

Phillis, an adult slave belonging to William Hudgins, was born in March 1777 and was baptized on May 4, 1777. Kingston Parish Register, p. 87.

Philly, a slave belonging to John Read's estate, was born on March 29, 1750. Kingston Parish Register, p. 103.

Philly, a slave belonging to John Read's estate, was baptized on June 24, 1750. Kingston Parish Register, p. 42.

Pollipus, Tom. See Tom Pollipus.

Polly, a slave belonging to Capt. William Hayes, was born on June 2, 1768. Kingston Parish Register, p. 65.

Polly, a slave belonging to Capt. Thomas Smith, was born on April 11, 1772, and was baptized on June 21, 1772. Kingston Parish Register, p. 65.

Polly, a slave belonging to Walter Keeble, was born on March 15, 1773, and was baptized on April 12, 1773. Kingston Parish Register, p. 74.

Polly, a slave belonging to John Page of Ware Parish, was born in June 1774 and was baptized on August 7, 1774. Kingston Parish Register, p. 78.

Primus, a slave belonging to Kemp Whiting, was born on December 18, 1759. Kingston Parish Register, p. 51.

Primus, a 9-year-old slave whose owner's name was omitted from the parish register, was baptized on August 16, 1772. Kingston Parish Register, p. 71.

Primus, an adult slave belonging to Daniel Williams, was baptized on September 13, 1772. Kingston Parish Register, p. 72.

Prince, a slave belonging to Mr. Armistead, was baptized on April 15, 1750. Kingston Parish Register, p. 41.

Prince, a slave belonging to Joseph King, was baptized on September 8, 1772. Kingston Parish Register, p. 70.

Prince, a slave belonging to John Hayes, was baptized on July 4, 1773. Kingston Parish Register, p. 75.

Prince, a slave belonging to Robert Matthews, was born in March 1774 and was baptized on May 8, 1774. Kingston Parish Register, p. 77.

Priscilla, a slave belonging to William Armistead Esq., was born in September 1775 and was baptized on December 1, 1775. Kingston Parish Register, p. 83.

R

Rachel, a slave belonging to Mr. Debman, was baptized on March 11, 1750. Kingston Parish Register, p. 41.

Rachel, a slave belonging to Richard Hunley, was baptized on September 2, 1750. Kingston Parish Register, p. 42.

Rachel, a slave belonging to Peter Wyatt, was born on April 19, 1756. Kingston Parish Register, p. 47.

Rachel, a slave belonging to William Hayes, was born in December 1757. Kingston Parish Register, p. 49.

Rachel, a slave belonging to John Gwyn, was born on December 14, 1760. Kingston Parish Register, p. 53.

Rachel, a slave belonging to John Davis, was born on June 23, 1762. Kingston Parish Register, p. 55.

Rachel, a slave belonging to Elizabeth Lux, was born in July 1764. Kingston Parish Register, p. 59.

Rachel, a slave belonging to Elizabeth Billups, was born on September 28, 1765. Kingston Parish Register, p. 61.

Rachel, a slave belonging to Robert Billups, was born on June 7, 1767. Kingston Parish Register, p. 63.

Rachel, a slave belonging to Edmund Borum, was born on June 20, 1767. Kingston Parish Register, p. 63.

Rachel, a slave belonging to Major William Plummer, was born on September 1, 1767. Kingston Parish Register, p. 63.

Rachel, a slave belonging to Lucy Gwyn, was born on March 6, 1771, and was baptized on May 20, 1771. Kingston Parish Register, p. 67.

Rachel, a slave belonging to Christopher Cully, was born on April 25, 1771, and was baptized on June 9, 1771. Kingston Parish Register, p. 67.

Rachel, a slave belonging to Mrs. Tabb, was baptized on November 3, 1772. Kingston Parish Register, p. 70.

Rachel, a slave belonging to Thomas Respess, was born in August 1773 and was baptized on December 12, 1773. Kingston Parish Register, p. 76.

Rachel, a slave belonging to Thomas Davis, was born on August 29, 1773, and was baptized on October 24, 1773. Kingston Parish Register, p. 76.

Rachel, a slave belonging to Ann Matthews, was born in April 1774 and was baptized on May 15, 1774. Kingston Parish Register, p. 78.

Rachel, a slave belonging to Christopher Adams, was born in January 1775 and was baptized on March 19, 1775. Kingston Parish Register, p. 80.

Ralph, a slave belonging to Ann Ransone, was born on June 15, 1753. Kingston Parish Register, p. 44.

Ralph, a slave belonging to Charles Blacknall, was born in November 1754. Kingston Parish Register, p. 45.

Ralph, a slave belonging to Robert Hunley, was born on April 19, 1757. Kingston Parish Register, p. 48.

Ralph, a slave belonging to John Gayle, was born in October 1757. Kingston Parish Register, p. 49.

Ralph, a slave belonging to William Tompkins, was born on November 1, 1760. Kingston Parish Register, p. 53.

Ralph, a slave belonging to Robert Bristow's estate, was born on July 29, 1768. Kingston Parish Register, p. 65.

Ralph, a slave belonging to Robert Foster, was born on April 21, 1769. Kingston Parish Register, p. 65.

Ralph, a slave belonging to Mr. R. Spencer, was born on November 4, 1770. Kingston Parish Register, p. 66.

Ralph, a slave belonging to Gabriel Hughes, was born in 1772 and was baptized on January 24, 1773. Kingston Parish Register, p. 73.

Ralph, a slave belonging to James Hunley, was born on August 12, 1773, and was baptized on September 12, 1773. Kingston Parish Register, p. 76.

Ralph, an adult slave belonging to William Merchant, was baptized on September 25, 1774. Kingston Parish Register, p. 79.

Ralph, a slave belonging to Humphrey Hudgins, was born on March 10, 1775, and was baptized on February 26, 1775. Kingston Parish Register, p. 80.

Ralph, a slave belonging to Humphrey Hudgins, was born on March 10, 1775, and was baptized on March 26, 1775. Kingston Parish Register, p. 81.

Ralph, a slave belonging to William Jarvis, was born on February 29, 1776, and was baptized on March 10, 1776. Kingston Parish Register, p. 84.

Ralph, a slave belonging to James Thomas, was born on April 1, 1777, and was baptized on June 1, 1777. Kingston Parish Register, p. 88.

Randolph, a slave belonging to Sir John Peyton, was born on November 4, 1770. Kingston Parish Register, p. 66.

Rebecca, a slave belonging to Capt. George Dudley, was baptized on April 16, 1750. Kingston Parish Register, p. 41.

Rebecca, a slave belonging to Elizabeth Jones, was born in May 1775 and was baptized on July 9, 1775. Kingston Parish Register, p. 82.

Reuben, a male slave belonging to Major Kemp Plummer, was born in March 1771 and was baptized on April 14, 1771. Kingston Parish Register, p. 67.

Reuben, a slave belonging to Capt. John Billups, was born on August 16, 1772, and was baptized on September 13, 1772. Kingston Parish Register, p. 67.

Reuben, a slave belonging to Major William Plummer, was born on June 1, 1773, and was baptized on August 1, 1773. Kingston Parish Register, p. 76.

Reuben, a slave belonging to Ann Hodges, was born in March 1774 and was baptized on April 17, 1774. Kingston Parish Register, p. 77.

Reuben, a slave belonging to Robert Spencer, was born in late 1775 or early 1776 and was baptized on January 21, 1776. Kingston Parish Register, p. 84.

Reuben, a slave belonging to John Hayes, was born on March 28, 1776, and was baptized on May 5, 1776. Kingston Parish Register, p. 85.

Reynolds or Rinolds, a slave belonging to Richard Hunley, was baptized on May 13, 1750. Kingston Parish Register, p. 42.

Richard, a slave belonging to William Hayes, was baptized on April 22, 1750. Kingston Parish Register, p. 41.

Richard, a slave belonging to Eleanor Lewis, was baptized on April 29, 1750. Kingston Parish Register, p. 41.

Richard, a slave belonging to Major Dudley, was baptized on April 29, 1750. Kingston Parish Register, p. 41.

Richard, a slave belonging to the Rev. John Dixon, was born in May 1758. Kingston Parish Register, p. 49.

Richard, a slave belonging to Elizabeth Holder, was born on October 29, 1758. Kingston Parish Register, p. 50.

Richard, a slave belonging to William Callis, was born on February 29, 1759. Kingston Parish Register, p. 50.

Richard, a slave belonging to John Armistead, was born on May 16, 1762. Kingston Parish Register, p. 55.

Richard, a slave belonging to Susannah Iverson, was born on August 25, 1763. Kingston Parish Register, p. 57.

Richard, a slave belonging to Ambrose Merchant, was born in May 1766. Kingston Parish Register, p. 62.

Richard, a slave belonging to John Foster, was born on August 31, 1766. Kingston Parish Register, p. 62.

Richard, a slave belonging to John Gwyn, was born in November 1767. Kingston Parish Register, p. 64.

Richard, a slave belonging to John Hurst, was born on June 22, 1769. Kingston Parish Register, p. 65.

Richard, a slave belonging to Thomas Hayes, was born on July 6, 1769. Kingston Parish Register, p. 66.

Richard, an adult slave belonging to the Widow Hunley, was baptized in 1772. Kingston Parish Register, p. 70.

Richard, a slave belonging to Joseph Billups, was born on February 4, 1772, and was baptized on March 1, 1772. Kingston Parish Register, p. 69.

Richard, an adult slave belonging to Gabriel Miller, was baptized on September 13, 1772. Kingston Parish Register, p. 72.

Richard, an adult slave belonging to James Hunley, was baptized on September 13, 1772. Kingston Parish Register, p. 72.

Richard, a slave belonging to Capt. Thomas Smith, was born on October 31, 1772, and was baptized on December 6, 1772. Kingston Parish Register, p. 71.

Richard, a slave belonging to Harry Gwyn, was born in late 1772 or early 1773 and was baptized on January 31, 1773. Kingston Parish Register, p. 73.

Richard, a slave belonging to Robert Billups, was born in February 1773 and was baptized on May 2, 1773. Kingston Parish Register, p. 74.

Richard, a slave belonging to the Rev. John Dixon, was born on February 13, 1773, and was baptized on February 15, 1773. Kingston Parish Register, p. 73.

Richard, a slave belonging to George Brooks, was born on May 1, 1774, and was baptized on June 5, 1774. Kingston Parish Register, p. 78.

Richard, a slave belonging to John Billups, was born on September 2, 1774, and was baptized on October 23, 1774. Kingston Parish Register, p. 79.

Richard, a slave belonging to Jacob Hackney, was born in March 1775 and was baptized on April 30, 1775. Kingston Parish Register, p. 81.

Richard, a slave belonging to Robert Armistead, was born in May 1775 and was baptized on July 2, 1775. Kingston Parish Register, p. 82.

Richard, a slave belonging to John King, was born in April 1776 and was baptized on June 23, 1776. Kingston Parish Register, p. 85.

Richard James, a slave belonging to Harry Gwyn, was born in February 1768. Kingston Parish Register, p. 64.

Robert, a slave belonging to Mr. Armistead, was baptized on April 15, 1750. Kingston Parish Register, p. 41.

Robert, a slave belonging to William Hayes, was baptized on May 13, 1750. Kingston Parish Register, p. 41.

Robert, a slave belonging to John Foster, was born on March 10, 1760. Kingston Parish Register, p. 52.

Robert, a slave belonging to Harry Gwyn, was born in October 1766. Kingston Parish Register, p. 62.

Robert, a slave belonging to John Tompkins, was born in 1772 and was baptized on January 10, 1773. Kingston Parish Register, p. 73.

Robert, a slave belonging to Letitia Ransone, was born in March 1777 and was baptized on April 6, 1777. Kingston Parish Register, p. 87.

Robin, a slave belonging to Thomas Smith, was born in May 1756. Kingston Parish Register, p. 47.

Robin, a slave belonging to Bristow's estate, was born on April 24, 1759. Kingston Parish Register, p. 51.

Robin, a slave belonging to Elizabeth Billups, was born on August 4, 1763. Kingston Parish Register, p. 57.

Robin, a slave belonging to Walter Keeble, was born on April 30, 1765. Kingston Parish Register, p. 60.

Robin, a slave belonging to Capt. William Hayes' estate, was born on June 6, 1771, and was baptized on October 13, 1771. Kingston Parish Register, p. 68.

Robin, a slave belonging to William Callis, was born in July 1771 and was baptized on October 13, 1771. Kingston Parish Register, p. 68.

Robin, a slave belonging to Robert Green, was baptized on November 3, 1772. Kingston Parish Register, p. 70.

Robin, a slave belonging to Mary Hudgins, was born on May 7, 1773, and was baptized on July 4, 1773. Kingston Parish Register, p. 75.

Robin, a slave belonging to Mary Digges, was born on June 30, 1775, and was baptized on July 16, 1775. Kingston Parish Register, p. 82.

Robin, a slave belonging to Mary Digges, was born on June 30, 1775, and was baptized on July 16, 1775. Kingston Parish Register, p. 83.

Robin, an adult slave belonging to Robert Armistead, was baptized on July 16, 1775. Kingston Parish Register, p. 82.

Roger, a slave belonging to James Davis, was born on May 19, 1763. Kingston Parish Register, p. 57.

Roger, a slave belonging to George Brown, was born on July 14, 1763. Kingston Parish Register, p. 57.

Roger, an adult slave belonging to Robert Cully, was baptized on September 13, 1772. Kingston Parish Register, p. 72.

Rosanna, an adult slave belonging to Joseph Miller, was baptized on September 13, 1772. Kingston Parish Register, p. 72.

Rosanna, an adult slave belonging to James Hunley, was baptized on September 13, 1772. Kingston Parish Register, p. 72.

Rose, a slave belonging to William Elliott, was born on March 11, 1750. Kingston Parish Register, p. 41.

Rose, a slave girl belonging to Edmund Borum, was born on August 4, 1751. Kingston Parish Register, p. 43.

Rose, a slave belonging to Francis Armistead, was born in January 1756. Kingston Parish Register, p. 47.

Rose, a slave belonging to Robert Billups, was born on May 28, 1756. Kingston Parish Register, p. 47.

Rose, a slave belonging to Capt. Thomas Machen, was born in June 1757. Kingston Parish Register, p. 48.

Rose, a slave belonging to Joannah Miller, was born on June 5, 1759. Kingston Parish Register, p. 51.

Rose, a slave belonging to Capt. Thomas Smith, was born on January 11, 1763. Kingston Parish Register, p. 56.

Rose, a slave belonging to William Hayes, was born on July 15, 1764. Kingston Parish Register, p. 59.

Rose, a slave belonging to James Harper, was born on April 8, 1766. Kingston Parish Register, p. 61.

Rose, a slave belonging to Capt. William Hayes' estate, was born on June 6, 1771, and was baptized on July 7, 1771. Kingston Parish Register, p. 68.

Rose, a slave belonging to John Gayle, was born on March 1, 1772, and was baptized on July 7, 1771. Kingston Parish Register, p. 69.

Rose, a slave belonging to James Peade, was born in April 1774 and was baptized on June 5, 1774. Kingston Parish Register, p. 78.

Rose, a slave belonging to Frances Tabb, was born in April 1774 and was baptized on June 12, 1774. Kingston Parish Register, p. 78.

Rose, a slave belonging to John Hudgins, was born on July 12, 1774, and was baptized on August 28, 1774. Kingston Parish Register, p. 78.

Rose, a slave belonging to John Tompkins, was born in August 1774 and was baptized on October 30, 1774. Kingston Parish Register, p. 79.

Rose, a slave belonging to Judith Plummer, was born in January 1775 and was baptized on March 19, 1775. Kingston Parish Register, p. 80.

Rose, a slave belonging to Peter Smith, was born in July 1776 and was baptized on August 11, 1776. Kingston Parish Register, p. 86.

Rose, a slave belonging to Widow Jones, was born in August 1777 and was baptized on October 26, 1777. Kingston Parish Register, p. 89.

Rose, a slave belonging to James Davis, was born on August 9, 1777, and was baptized on October 19, 1777. Kingston Parish Register, p. 89.

Rose and Visa, twin slaves belonging to Andrew Kerr, were born on June 1, 1777, and were baptized on June 29, 1777. Kingston Parish Register, p. 88.

Rosy, a slave belonging to Widow Jones, was baptized on May 20, 1750. Kingston Parish Register, p. 42.

S

Sall, a slave belonging to Susanna Tabb, was born on August 1, 1773, and was baptized on December 12, 1773. Kingston Parish Register, p. 76.

Sall, a slave belonging to Sir John Peyton, was born in April 1776 and was baptized on June 23, 1776. Kingston Parish Register, p. 85.

Sally, a slave belonging to Walter Keeble, was born in March 1763. Kingston Parish Register, p. 56.

Sally or Salley, a slave belonging to Esther Hunley, was born on February 20, 1764. Kingston Parish Register, p. 58.

Sally or Salley, a slave belonging to Bristow's estate, was born on July 18, 1764. Kingston Parish Register, p. 59.

Sally or Salley, a slave belonging to Humphrey Billups, was born on August 1, 1764. Kingston Parish Register, p. 59.

Sally or Salley, a slave belonging to Humphrey Billups, was born on November 30, 1765. Kingston Parish Register, p. 61.

Sally or Salley, a slave belonging to Capt. William Hayes, was born on June 28, 1766. Kingston Parish Register, p. 62.

Sally, a slave belonging to William Lilly, was born on March 28, 1768. Kingston Parish Register, p. 64.

Sally, a slave belonging to Sarah Smith, was born in February 1769. Kingston Parish Register, p. 65.

Sally, a slave belonging to Capt. Thomas Smith, was born on November 2, 1770. Kingston Parish Register, p. 66.

Sally, a slave belonging to George Armistead, was born on September 26, 1771, and was baptized on October 27, 1771. Kingston Parish Register, p. 68.

Sally, a slave belonging to Ambrose Merchant, was born in June 1772 and was baptized on August 16, 1772. Kingston Parish Register, p. 71.

Sally, a slave belonging to Andrew Kerr, was born on August 10, 1772, and was baptized on September 13, 1772. Kingston Parish Register, p. 71.

Sally, a slave belonging to John Ripley, was born on June 3, 1773, and was baptized on July 4, 1773. Kingston Parish Register, p. 75

Sally, an adult slave belonging to Langley Billups' widow, was baptized on July 4, 1773. Kingston Parish Register, p. 75.

Sally, a slave belonging to Humphrey Davis, was born on December 20, 1773, and was baptized on February 27, 1774. Kingston Parish Register, p. 77.

Sally, a slave belonging to Humphrey Hudgins, was born in March 1774 and was baptized on March 13, 1774. Kingston Parish Register, p. 77.

Sally, a slave belonging to Robert Billups, was born in March 1774 and was baptized on May 8, 1774. Kingston Parish Register, p. 77.

Sally, a slave belonging to Major John Robinson, was born in April 1774 and was baptized on June 12, 1774. Kingston Parish Register, p. 78.

Sally, a slave belonging to John Elliott, was born in August 1774 and was baptized on September 18, 1774. Kingston Parish Register, p. 79.

Sally, a slave belonging to Augustine Curtis, was born in August 1774 and was baptized on October 30, 1774. Kingston Parish Register, p. 79.

Sally, an adult slave belonging to the Widow Hudgins, was baptized on December 26, 1774. Kingston Parish Register, p. 80.

Sally, a slave belonging to Capt. John Billups, was born in March 1775 and was baptized on March 26, 1775. Kingston Parish Register, p. 81.

Sally, a slave belonging to Robert Matthews, was born in May 1775 and was baptized on July 9, 1775. Kingston Parish Register, p. 82.

Sally, a slave belonging to James Harper, was born in June 1776 and was baptized on July 14, 1776. Kingston Parish Register, p. 85.

Sally, a slave belonging to George Alexander Dudley, was born in June 1777 and was baptized on July 6, 1777. Kingston Parish Register, p. 88.

Sally, a slave belonging to Robert Armistead, was born on June 27, 1777, and was baptized on July 27, 1777. Kingston Parish Register, p. 88.

Sam, a slave belonging to Capt. Whiting, was born on April 3, 1750. Kingston Parish Register, p. 103.

Sam, a slave belonging to William Bond, was born on June 22, 1756. Kingston Parish Register, p. 47.

Sam, a slave belonging to George Hunley, was born in March 1757. Kingston Parish Register, p. 48.

Sam, a slave belonging to Capt. William Hayes, was born on June 19, 1763. Kingston Parish Register, p. 57.

Sam, a slave belonging to Major Kemp Plummer, was born on March 8, 1765. Kingston Parish Register, p. 60.

Sam, a slave belonging to Sir John Peyton, was born on September 12, 1773, and was baptized on December 12, 1773. Kingston Parish Register, p. 76.

Sam, a slave belonging to Richard Hurst, was born on June 17, 1774, and was baptized on July 17, 1774. Kingston Parish Register, p. 78.

Sam, a slave belonging to William Merchant, was born in March 1775 and was baptized on April 2, 1775. Kingston Parish Register, p. 81.

Sam, a slave belonging to Major Thomas Smith, was born in March 1776 and was baptized on June 16, 1776. Kingston Parish Register, p. 85.

Sam, a slave belonging to Thomas Hayes, was born on April 18, 1776, and was baptized on June 16, 1776. Kingston Parish Register, p. 85.

Sampson or Samson, a slave belonging to Robert Bernard, was born in July 1760. Kingston Parish Register, p. 52.

Sampson, a slave belonging to Ann Thomas, was born in May 1763. Kingston Parish Register, p. 57.

Sampson, a slave belonging to John Nuttall, was born on June 7, 1767. Kingston Parish Register, p. 63.

Sampson, a slave belonging to William Lilly, was born on April 25, 1772, and was baptized on June 21, 1772. Kingston Parish Register, p. 69.

Sampson or Samson, an adult slave belonging to Francis Armistead, was baptized on September 13, 1772. Kingston Parish Register, p. 72.

Sampson, a slave belonging to William Armistead, was born in late 1772 or early 1773 and was baptized on February 7, 1773. Kingston Parish Register, p. 73.

Sampson, a slave belonging to Mrs. Lux, was born in 1773 and was baptized on February 6, 1774. Kingston Parish Register, p. 77.

Sampson, an adult slave belonging to William Merchant, was baptized on September 25, 1774. Kingston Parish Register, p. 79.

Samuel, a slave belonging to William Elliott, was baptized on March 11, 1750. Kingston Parish Register, p. 41.

Samuel, a slave belonging to Mr. Debman, was baptized on March 11, 1750. Kingston Parish Register, p. 41.

Samuel, a slave belonging to Mrs. Ann Armistead, was born on August 23, 1758. Kingston Parish Register, p. 50.

Samuel, a slave belonging to Charles Blacknall, was born on March 11, 1760. Kingston Parish Register, p. 52.

Samuel, a slave belonging to William Armistead Esq., was born in September 1775 and was baptized on December 1, 1775. Kingston Parish Register, p. 83.

Sander, a slave belonging to Robert Read, was born on May 20. 1754. Kingston Parish Register, p. 45.

Sarah, a slave belonging to Capt. George Dudley, was baptized on April 16, 1750. Kingston Parish Register, p. 41.

Sarah, a slave belonging to Mrs. Ann Armistead, was baptized on April 29, 1750. Kingston Parish Register, p. 41.

Sarah, a slave belonging to Richard Hunley, was baptized on May 13, 1750. Kingston Parish Register, p. 42.

Sarah, a slave belonging to Letitia Ransone, was baptized on September 2, 1750. Kingston Parish Register, p. 42.

Sarah, a slave belonging to John Hayes, was baptized on September 16, 1750. Kingston Parish Register, p. 42.

Sarah, a slave belonging to John Cary Jr., was born on June 14, 1753. Kingston Parish Register, p. 44.

Sarah, a slave belonging to James Callis Jr., was born on December 24, 1758. Kingston Parish Register, p. 50.

Sarah, a slave belonging to James Ransone, was born on September 20, 1759. Kingston Parish Register, p. 51.

Sarah, a slave belonging to Major Kemp Plummer, was born in December 1761. Kingston Parish Register, p. 55.

Sarah, a slave belonging to Isaac Smith, was born on November 12, 1762. Kingston Parish Register, p. 56.

Sarah, a slave belonging to Major Kemp Plummer, was born in December 1762. Kingston Parish Register, p. 56.

Sarah, a slave belonging to Catherine Spencer, was born on March 9, 1763. Kingston Parish Register, p. 56.

Sarah, a slave belonging to William Hudgins, was born on August 15, 1763. Kingston Parish Register, p. 57.

Sarah, a slave belonging to William Callis, was born on December 25, 1763. Kingston Parish Register, p. 58.

Sarah, a slave belonging to James Davis, was born in March 1764. Kingston Parish Register, p. 58.

Sarah, a slave belonging to Robert Read, was born in April 1766. Kingston Parish Register, p. 61.

Sarah, a slave belonging to Edward Anderson, was born on June 23, 1766. Kingston Parish Register, p. 62.

Sarah, a slave belonging to Matthias James, was born on November 10, 1766. Kingston Parish Register, p. 62.

Sarah, a slave belonging to Major Kemp Plummer, was born on September 26, 1767. Kingston Parish Register, p. 63.

Sarah, a slave belonging to Robert Billups, was born in January 1768. Kingston Parish Register, p. 64.

Sarah, a slave belonging to Thomas Hayes, was born in April 1769. Kingston Parish Register, p. 65.

Sarah, a slave belonging to Christopher Dawson, was born in June 1769. Kingston Parish Register, p. 65.

Sarah, a slave belonging to Capt. Francis Armistead, was born on June 24, 1769. Kingston Parish Register, p. 65.

Sarah, a slave belonging to Dawson Eddins, was born in October 1769. Kingston Parish Register, p. 66.

Sarah, a slave belonging to Augustine Curtis, was baptized on November 3, 1772. Kingston Parish Register, p. 70.

Sarah, a slave belonging to Daniel Williams, was born on October 18, 1773, and was baptized on December 5, 1773. Kingston Parish Register, p. 76.

Sarah, an adult slave belonging to Sir John Peyton, was baptized on March 23, 1775. Kingston Parish Register, p. 80.

Sarah, a slave belonging to Elizabeth Holder, was born in October 1775 and was baptized on December 17, 1775. Kingston Parish Register, p. 83.

Sarah, a slave belonging to John Billups, was born in March 1776 and was baptized on May 5, 1776. Kingston Parish Register, p. 85.

Sarah and Charles, adult slaves belonging to William Merchant, were born in April 1777 and were baptized on June 15, 1777. Kingston Parish Register, p. 88.

Sarah, a slave belonging to Thomas Iverson's estate, was born in May 1777 and was baptized on June 1, 1777. Kingston Parish Register, p. 88.

Scilla, a slave belonging to Christopher Gayle, was born on April 1, 1770. Kingston Parish Register, p. 66.

Scilla, a slave belonging to Capt. William Hayes, was born on May 13, 1770. Kingston Parish Register, p. 66.

Scilla, a female slave belonging to Major Kemp Plummer, was born in March 1771 and was baptized on April 14, 1771. Kingston Parish Register, p. 67.

Scilla, a slave belonging to Rose Anna Lilly, was born on May 17, 1771, and was baptized on June 23, 1771. Kingston Parish Register, p. 68.

Scilla, a slave belonging to Ambrose Merchant, was born in May 1772 and was baptized on August 16, 1772. Kingston Parish Register, p. 71.

Scilla, a slave belonging to William Elliott, was born in February 1773 and was baptized on May 16, 1773. Kingston Parish Register, p. 74.

Scilla, a slave belonging to Henry Forrest, was born in June 1775 and was baptized on July 2, 1775. Kingston Parish Register, p. 82.

Scilla, a slave belonging to Matthias James, was born in October 1775 and was baptized on December 17, 1755. Kingston Parish Register, p. 83.

Scipio, a slave belonging to Josiah Foster, was born in April 1776 and was baptized on June 16, 1776. Kingston Parish Register, p. 85.

Seaton, a slave belonging to Ann Hunley, was born on September 21, 1756. Kingston Parish Register, p. 47.

Si or Li, a slave belonging to Richard Hunley, was baptized on September 2, 1750. Kingston Parish Register, p. 42.

Si, a slave belonging to Daniel Williams, was born on July 21, 1771, and was baptized on August 18, 1771. Kingston Parish Register, p. 68.

Si, a slave belonging to Sir John Peyton, was born in late 1775 or early 1776 and was baptized on February 18, 1776. Kingston Parish Register, p. 84.

Sidney, a slave belonging to Matthew Whiting, was born in May 1771 and was baptized on June 9, 1771. Kingston Parish Register, p. 68.

Sil, a slave belonging to John Billups, was born on April 20, 1761. Kingston Parish Register, p. 54.

Siller, a slave belonging to Capt. Robert Whiting, was born on October 2, 1754. Kingston Parish Register, p. 45.

Siller, a slave belonging to John Cary Sr., was born on April 3, 1764. Kingston Parish Register, p. 58.

Siller, a slave belonging to Joseph Gayle, was born on July 29, 1764. Kingston Parish Register, p. 59.

Siller, a slave belonging to Joseph Gayle, was born on December 18, 1765. Kingston Parish Register, p. 61.

Siller, a slave belonging to John Foster Jr., was born on July 1, 1769. Kingston Parish Register, p. 66.

Silva, a slave belonging to Kemp Plummer, was born in January 1759. Kingston Parish Register, p. 50.

Silvia, a slave belonging to Thomas Billups, was born in February 1777 and was baptized on March 9, 1777. Kingston Parish Register, p. 87.

Silvy, a slave belonging to Elizabeth Lewis, was born on October 20, 1767. Kingston Parish Register, p. 64.

Simon, a 7-year-old slave associated with the Kingston Parish glebe, was baptized on November 26, 1749. Kingston Parish Register, p. 41.

Simon, a slave belonging to William Tabb, was baptized on July 1, 1750. Kingston Parish Register, p. 42.

Simon, a slave belonging to Thomas Machen, was born on December 26, 1754. Kingston Parish Register, p. 46.

Simon, a slave belonging to Charles Blacknall, was born in April 1759. Kingston Parish Register, p. 51.

Simon, a slave belonging to Thomas Hayes Jr., was born on June 22, 1761. Kingston Parish Register, p. 54.

Simon, a slave belonging to James Ransone, was born on October 10, 1761. Kingston Parish Register, p. 54.

Simon, a slave belonging to Mary Blacknall, was born on April 24, 1768. Kingston Parish Register, p. 64.

Simon, a slave belonging to George William Plummer, was born on September 4, 1773, and was baptized on September 26, 1773. Kingston Parish Register, p. 76.

Simon, a slave belonging to Sir John Peyton, was born in September 1775 and was baptized on November 25, 1775. Kingston Parish Register, p. 83.

Simon, a slave belonging to Dorothy Cary, was born in late 1775 or early 1776 and was baptized on March 3, 1776. Kingston Parish Register, p. 84.

Smith, John. See John Smith.

Solomon, a slave belonging to Major Robert Bristow's estate, was born on October 15, 1754. Kingston Parish Register, p. 45.

Solomon, a slave belonging to Charles Blacknall, was born in November 1754. Kingston Parish Register, p. 45.

Solomon, a slave belonging to James Davis, was born on March 30, 1761. Kingston Parish Register, p. 54.

Solomon, an adult slave belonging to James Cray, was baptized on September 13, 1772. Kingston Parish Register, p. 72.

Sparkley Green, a slave belonging to Sir John Peyton, was born in December 1770 and was baptized on January 27, 1771. Kingston Parish Register, p. 67.

Spencer, a slave belonging to Matthias James, was born in July 1770. Kingston Parish Register, p. 66.

Sprig, a slave belonging to Charles Blacknall, was baptized on September 30, 1750. Kingston Parish Register, p. 42.

Sprig, a slave belonging to Humphrey Gwyn, was born on March 24, 1772, and was baptized on May 2, 1773. Kingston Parish Register, p. 69.

Sprig, a slave boy belonging to Francis Tabb, was born in March 1774 and was baptized on April 17, 1774. Kingston Parish Register, p. 77.

Sprig, a slave belonging to Mary Blacknall, was born in May 1775 and was baptized on June 18, 1775. Kingston Parish Register, p. 81.

Sprig, a slave belonging to John Willis, was born on May 7, 1775, and was baptized on June 18, 1775. Kingston Parish Register, p. 81.

Sprig, Anthony. See Anthony Sprig.

Sprig, Frank. See Frank Sprig.

Stephen, a slave belonging to Capt. William Hayes, was born on November 27, 1763. Kingston Parish Register, p. 58.

~~Sterling, a slave belonging to Lucy Machen, was born on October 10, 1764.~~ Kingston Parish Register, p. 59. *Note: a line was drawn through this entry.*

Sue and Tony, slave twins belonging to Caleb Hunley, were baptized on January 26, 1755. Kingston Parish Register, p. 46.

Sue, a slave belonging to James Ransone, was born on October 10, 1764. Kingston Parish Register, p. 59.

Sue, a slave belonging to Langley Billups, was born on December 25, 1768. Kingston Parish Register, p. 65.

Sue, a slave belonging to Augustine Curtis, was born in March 1771 and was baptized on April 21, 1771. Kingston Parish Register, p. 67.

Sue, a slave belonging to Augustine Curtis, was baptized on April 21, 1771. Kingston Parish Register, p. 70.

Sue, a slave belonging to John King, was born in February 1773 and was baptized on April 4, 1773. Kingston Parish Register, p. 73.

Sue, a slave belonging to James Harper, was born on May 1, 1773, and was baptized on June 20, 1773. Kingston Parish Register, p. 74.

Sue, a slave belonging to Robert Cully, was born on August 2, 1773, and was baptized on October 24, 1773. Kingston Parish Register, p. 76.

Sue, an adult slave belonging to Mr. Borum, was baptized on September 25, 1774. Kingston Parish Register, p. 79.

Sue, a slave belonging to Isaac Smith, was born in March 1776 and was baptized on May 5, 1776. Kingston Parish Register, p. 85.

Sukey, a slave belonging to William Hayes, was born in August 1758. Kingston Parish Register, p. 50.

Sukey, a slave belonging to Elizabeth Lilly, was born in August 1761. Kingston Parish Register, p. 54.

Sukey, a slave belonging to Gabriel Hughes, was born on August 8, 1764. Kingston Parish Register, p. 59.

Sukey, a slave belonging to John Gayle, was born in November 1766. Kingston Parish Register, p. 62.

Sukey, a slave belonging to Currel Armistead, was born on July 16, 1768. Kingston Parish Register, p. 65.

Sukey, a slave belonging to Elizabeth Holder, was born on October 20, 1775, and was baptized on December 17, 1775. Kingston Parish Register, p. 83.

Sukey, a slave belonging to Sir John Peyton, was born in April 1776 and was baptized on June 23, 1776. Kingston Parish Register, p. 85.

Susanna, a slave belonging to Mr. Brooks, was baptized on June 24, 1750. Kingston Parish Register, p. 42.

Susanna or Susannah, a slave belonging to William Lilly, was born on December 26, 1764. Kingston Parish Register, p. 59.

Susanna or Susannah, a slave belonging to John Roots, was born on May 21, 1766. Kingston Parish Register, p. 62.

Susanna, a slave belonging to James Davis, was born on May 31, 1769. Kingston Parish Register, p. 65.

Susanna, an adult slave belonging to Thomas Jones, was baptized in 1772. Kingston Parish Register, p. 70.

Susanna, a slave belonging to Christopher Gayle's estate, was born on July 19, 1772, and was baptized on September 13, 1772. Kingston Parish Register, p. 71.

Susanna, a slave belonging to Anna Billups, was born on April 30, 1773, and was baptized on July 4, 1773. Kingston Parish Register, p. 74.

Susanna, a slave belonging to Augustine Digges, was born on May 15, 1773, and was baptized on July 4, 1773. Kingston Parish Register, p.75.

Susanna, a slave belonging to Isaac Smith, was born on May 22, 1773, and was baptized on July 4, 1773. Kingston Parish Register, p. 75.

Susanna, a slave belonging to Joseph Miller, was born in April 1773 and was baptized on March 13, 1774. Kingston Parish Register, p. 77.

Susanna, a slave belonging to Thomas Smith, was born on July 4, 1774, and was baptized on August 28, 1774. Kingston Parish Register, p. 78.

Susanna, a slave belonging to John Foster Sr., was born in March 1775 and was baptized on May 7, 1775. Kingston Parish Register, p. 81.

Sutton, a slave belonging to James Peade, was born on December 26, 1764. Kingston Parish Register, p. 58.

Sutton, a slave belonging to Frances Digges, was born on February 14, 1765. Kingston Parish Register, p. 60.

Sutton, a slave belonging to Francis Armistead, was born on December 30, 1765. Kingston Parish Register, p. 61.

Sutton, a slave belonging to Joseph Digges, was born on August 14, 1766. Kingston Parish Register, p. 62.

Sutton, a slave belonging to Francis Miller, was born on July 25, 1771, and was baptized on September 1, 1771. Kingston Parish Register, p. 68.

Sutton, a slave belonging to John Eddins, was born on September 23, 1774, and was baptized on November 20, 1774. Kingston Parish Register, p. 80.

T

Tabb, a slave belonging to Jane Carter, was born in February 1777 and was baptized on April 13, 1777. Kingston Parish Register, p. 87.

Tabb, Benjamin. See Benjamin Tabb.

Tamar or Tamer, a slave belonging to Hugh Gwyn, was baptized on April 29, 1750. Kingston Parish Register, p. 41.

Tamar or Tamer, a slave belonging to John Read, was baptized on April 29. 1750. Kingston Parish Register, p. 41.

Tamar or Tamer, a slave belonging to the Widow Gwyn, was baptized on April 29, 1750. Kingston Parish Register, p. 41.

Tamar or Tamer, a slave belonging to John Read's estate, was baptized on June 24, 1750. Kingston Parish Register, p. 42.

Tamar or Tamer, a slave belonging to Richard Merchant, was born on January 20, 1754. Kingston Parish Register, p. 45.

Tamar or Tamer, a slave belonging to John Eddins, was born on July 4, 1754. Kingston Parish Register, p. 45.

Tamar or Tamer, a slave belonging to Robert Hunley, was born on December 18, 1759. Kingston Parish Register, p. 51.

Tamar or Tamer, a slave belonging to Thomas Hayes, was born on January 4, 1764. Kingston Parish Register, p. 58.

Tamar or Tamer, a slave belonging to Josiah Foster, was born on October 30, 1765. Kingston Parish Register, p. 61.

Tamar or Tamer, a slave belonging to John Davis, was born on May 9, 1766. Kingston Parish Register, p. 62.

Tamar or Tamer, a slave belonging to Robert Billups, was born on August 15, 1766. Kingston Parish Register, p. 62.

Tamar or Tamer, a slave belonging to William Callis, was born in December 1768. Kingston Parish Register, p. 65.

Tamar or Tamer, a slave belonging to William Callis, was born on August 14, 1771, and was baptized on October 13, 1771. Kingston Parish Register, p. 68.

Tamar or Tamer, a slave belonging to Hugh Hayes, was born on September 11, 1772, and was baptized on October 11, 1772. Kingston Parish Register, p. 71.

Tamar, a slave belonging to James Thomas, was born in November 1773 and was baptized on May 8, 1774. Kingston Parish Register, p. 77.

Tamar, a slave belonging to William Hunley, was born in April 1773 and was baptized on March 13, 1774. Kingston Parish Register, p. 77.

Tamar, a slave belonging to Robert Cully, was born in July 1776 and was baptized on July 28, 1776. Kingston Parish Register, p. 85.

Tamar, a slave belonging to Humphrey Hudgins, was born in July 1776 and was baptized on September 22, 1776. Kingston Parish Register, p. 86.

Tawny, a slave belonging to John Cary Jr., died in January 1750. Kingston Parish Register, p. 179.

Thomas, a slave belonging to Richard Brown, was born on October 12, 1758. Kingston Parish Register, p. 50.

Thomas, a slave belonging to Robert Billups, was born on March 24, 1759. Kingston Parish Register, p. 50.

Thomas, a slave belonging to Thomas Hayes Jr., was born on July 22, 1768. Kingston Parish Register, p. 65.

Thomas, a slave belonging to Hugh Gwyn, was born in February 1773 and was baptized on May 2, 1773. Kingston Parish Register, p. 74.

Thomas, a slave belonging to Catherine Spencer, was born in March 1774 and was baptized on May 8, 1774. Kingston Parish Register, p. 77.

Thomas, a slave belonging to James Purcell, was born in March 1774 and was baptized on May 8, 1774. Kingston Parish Register, p. 77.

Thomas, a slave belonging to Mann Page Esq. of Ware Parish, was born in August 1774 and was baptized on October 30, 1774. Kingston Parish Register, p. 79.

Thomas Brown, a slave belonging to John Gwyn, died on December 27, 1753. Kingston Parish Register, p. 179.

Thomas Brown, a slave belonging to Richard [no last name], was born on October 12, 1758. Kingston Parish Register, p. 50.

Thomas Brown, a slave belonging to Capt. William Hayes, was born on July 23, 1764. Kingston Parish Register, p. 59.

Thomas Cooter, a slave belonging to John Davis, was born on February 3, 1767. Kingston Parish Register, p. 63.

Tim, an adult slave belonging to John King, was baptized on September 25, 1774. Kingston Parish Register, p. 79.

Tim, a slave belonging to Edward Hughes, was born in February 1776 and was baptized on April 14, 1776. Kingston Parish Register, p. 84.

Titus, a slave belonging to Major William Plummer, was born on July 4, 1767. Kingston Parish Register, p. 63.

Toby, a slave belonging to Capt. George Dudley, was baptized on April 16, 1750. Kingston Parish Register, p. 41.

Toby, a slave belonging to William White, was born on May 19, 1763. Kingston Parish Register, p. 57.

Toby, a slave belonging to John Armistead, was born on August 24, 1765. Kingston Parish Register, p. 60.

Toby, a slave belonging to William Bentley, was born on January 30, 1769. Kingston Parish Register, p. 65.

Tom, a slave belonging to James Ransone, was baptized on November 29, 1749. Kingston Parish Register, p. 42.

Tom, a slave belonging to John Jarvis, died on February 28, 1750. Kingston Parish Register, p. 103.

Tom, a slave belonging to Mr. Brooks' estate, was baptized on April 1, 1750. Kingston Parish Register, p. 41.

Tom, a slave belonging to Capt. George Dudley, was baptized on April 16, 1750. Kingston Parish Register, p. 41.

Tom, a slave boy belonging to the Rev. John Dixon, was born on March 1, 1753. Kingston Parish Register, p. 44.

Tom, a slave belonging to John Foster, was born on July 25, 1753. Kingston Parish Register, p. 44.

Tom, a slave belonging to John Keys, was born in October 1757. Kingston Parish Register, p. 49.

Tom, a slave belonging to James Davis, was born on July 20, 1760. Kingston Parish Register, p. 52.

Tom, a slave belonging to Capt. William Hayes, was born on January 1, 1761. Kingston Parish Register, p. 53.

Tom, a slave belonging to Harry Gwyn, was born on December 18, 1764. Kingston Parish Register, p. 59.

Tom, a slave belonging to Capt. Thomas Smith, was born on April 11, 1770. Kingston Parish Register, p. 66.

Tom, a slave belonging to John Armistead, was born on November 19, 1770. Kingston Parish Register, p. 66.

Tom, a slave belonging to John Armistead, was born on November 19, 1770, and was baptized on January 6, 1771. Kingston Parish Register, p. 67.

Tom, an adult slave belonging to Robert Matthews, was baptized in 1772. Kingston Parish Register, p. 70.

Tom, an adult slave belonging to Joseph Billups, was baptized on September 13, 1772. Kingston Parish Register, p. 72.

Tom, an adult slave belonging to William Respess, was baptized on September 13, 1772. Kingston Parish Register, p. 73.

Tom, a slave belonging to Isaac Smith, was born in March 1773 and was baptized on July 18, 1773. Kingston Parish Register, p. 75.

Tom, a slave belonging to Harry Gwyn, was born on June 13, 1773, and was baptized on July 18, 1773. Kingston Parish Register, p. 75.

Tom, an adult slave belonging to Andrew Kerr or Car, was baptized on July 4, 1773. Kingston Parish Register, p. 75.

Tom, a slave belonging to William Stevens, was born on June 20, 1775, and was baptized on July 16, 1775. Kingston Parish Register, pp. 75, 82.

Tom, a slave belonging to Joshua Gayle, was born in September or October 1776 and was baptized on December 1, 1776. Kingston Parish Register, p. 86.

Tom, a slave belonging to James Parsons, was born in late 1776 or early 1777 and was baptized on February 9, 1777. Kingston Parish Register, p. 87.

Tom Pollipus, a slave belonging to Mathew Whiting, was born on February 27, 1763. Kingston Parish Register, p. 56.

Tommy, a slave belonging to Joseph Billups, was born on July 25, 1762. Kingston Parish Register, p. 55.

Tony, a slave belonging to James Callis, was baptized on September 25, 1748. Kingston Parish Register, p. 42.

Tony, a slave belonging to Hugh Gwyn, was baptized on April 29, 1750. Kingston Parish Register, p. 41.

Tony, a slave belonging to Ann Ransone, was born on June 11, 1753. Kingston Parish Register, p. 44.

Tony and Sue, slave twins belonging to Caleb Hunley, were baptized on January 26, 1755. Kingston Parish Register, p. 46.

Tony, a slave belonging to John Cary Jr., was born on May 15, 1759. Kingston Parish Register, p. 51.

Tony, a slave belonging to James Ransone, was born on June 14, 1759. Kingston Parish Register, p. 51.

Tony, a slave belonging to John Gayle, was born in November 1760. Kingston Parish Register, p. 53.

Tony, an adult slave belonging to Daniel Williams, was baptized on August 30, 1772. Kingston Parish Register, p. 72.

Turner, a slave belonging to Jasper Clayton of Ware Parish, was born in February 1777 and was baptized on April 13, 1777. Kingston Parish Register, p. 87.

U

Unnamed male, a slave belonging to John Billups Sr., died on March 28, 1750. Kingston Parish Register, p. 103.

Unnamed male or female, a slave belonging to John Cary, died on April 18, 1750. Kingston Parish Register, p. 103.

Unnamed male or female, a slave belonging to Letitia Ransone, was born on June 19, 1768. Kingston Parish Register, p. 65.

Unnamed male or female, a slave belonging to Langley Billups' estate, was born on September 11, 1771, and was baptized on October 13, 1771. Kingston Parish Register, p. 68.

Ussie, a slave belonging to Capt. Gwyn Read's estate, was born in March 1766. Kingston Parish Register, p. 61.

V

Venus, a slave belonging to John Cary Sr., was born on June 29, 1753. Kingston Parish Register, p. 44.

Venus, a slave belonging to William White or Whitt, was born on August 19, 1761. Kingston Parish Register, p. 54.

Venus, a slave belonging to Richard Gwyn, was born on March 8, 1763. Kingston Parish Register, p. 56.

Venus, an adult slave belonging to Daniel Williams, was baptized on August 30, 1772. Kingston Parish Register, p. 72.

Venus, a slave belonging to Major William Plummer, was born in April 1773 and was baptized on July 18, 1773. Kingston Parish Register, p. 75.

Venus, a slave belonging to Mary Lowry, was born in June 1773 and was baptized on July 11, 1773. Kingston Parish Register, p. 75.

Visa and Rose, twin slaves belonging to Andrew Kerr, were born on June 1, 1777, and were baptized on June 29, 1777. Kingston Parish Register, p. 88.

Voss, an adult slave belonging to Sir John Peyton, was baptized on April 4, 1774. Kingston Parish Register, p. 77.

W

Waddy, a slave belonging to Thomas Hayes Jr., was born on July 15, 1767. Kingston Parish Register, p. 63.

Wapping, a slave belonging to Mrs. Mary Cunningham, was born on August 4, 1767. Kingston Parish Register, p. 103.

Warner, a slave belonging to Toy Tabb's estate, was baptized on November 17, 1772. Kingston Parish Register, p. 70.

Wharton, a slave belonging to Henry Gwyn, was born in August 1775 and was baptized on October 15, 1775. Kingston Parish Register, p. 83.

Will, a slave belonging to John Read's estate, was born on June 12, 1753. Kingston Parish Register, p. 44.

Will, a slave belonging to William Hayes, was born on April 22, 1755. Kingston Parish Register, p. 46.

Will, a slave belonging to Thomas Poole, was born on September 14, 1756. Kingston Parish Register, p. 47.

Will, a slave belonging to Robert Tompkins, was born on July 23, 1764. Kingston Parish Register, p. 59.

Will, an adult slave belonging to Joseph Billups, was baptized on July 4, 1777. Kingston Parish Register, p. 75.

Will, a slave belonging to Isaac Davis, was born on August 15, 1777, and was baptized on October 5, 1777. Kingston Parish Register, p. 88.

William, a slave belonging to John Hayes, was baptized on April 22, 1750. Kingston Parish Register, p. 41.

William, a slave belonging to Mr. Smith, was baptized on May 13, 1750. Kingston Parish Register, p. 42.

William, a slave belonging to Mr. Dawson, was baptized on June 24, 1750. Kingston Parish Register, p. 42.

William, a slave belonging to Capt. Kemp Plummer, was born in November 1757. Kingston Parish Register, p. 49.

William, a slave belonging to Major Kemp Plummer, was born on May 4, 1760. Kingston Parish Register, p. 52.

William, a slave belonging to Capt. William Hayes, was born on April 1, 1764. Kingston Parish Register, p. 58.

William, a slave belonging to Robert Bristow's estate, was born on April 12, 1767. Kingston Parish Register, p. 63.

William, a slave belonging to Joseph Billups, was born on July 18, 1768. Kingston Parish Register, p. 65.

William, a slave belonging to Capt. Francis Armistead, was born on June 4, 1769. Kingston Parish Register, p. 65.

William, a slave belonging to Capt. Thomas Smith, was born on July 27, 1769. Kingston Parish Register, p. 66.

William, a slave belonging to Thomas Lewis's estate, was born on January 2, 1770. Kingston Parish Register, p. 66.

William, a slave belonging to John Foster Jr., was born on February 2, 1771, and was baptized on April 14, 1771. Kingston Parish Register, p. 67.

William, a male slave belonging to Major Kemp Plummer, was born on March 1, 1771, and was baptized on April 14, 1771. Kingston Parish Register, p. 67.

William, a slave belonging to James Davis, was born in September 1771 and was baptized on April 26, 1772. Kingston Parish Register, p. 69.

William, an adult slave belonging to Robert Cully, was baptized on September 13, 1772. Kingston Parish Register, p. 72.

William, an adult slave belonging to Joseph Billups, was baptized on September 13, 1772. Kingston Parish Register, p. 72.

William, an adult slave belonging to John Davis, was baptized on September 13, 1772. Kingston Parish Register, p. 73.

William, a slave belonging to Christopher Adams, was born on April 11, 1773, and was baptized on May 9, 1773. Kingston Parish Register, p. 73.

William, an adult slave belonging to Langley Billups' widow, was baptized on July 4, 1773. Kingston Parish Register, p. 75.

William, a slave belonging to Mrs. Mary Blacknall, was born on August 3, 1773, and was baptized on September 12, 1773. Kingston Parish Register, p. 76.

William, a slave belonging to Sir John Peyton, was born on January 1, 1775, and was baptized on March 5, 1775. Kingston Parish Register, p. 80.

William, a slave belonging to Major Thomas Smith, was born on March 21, 1775, and was baptized on April 23, 1775. Kingston Parish Register, p. 81.

William, a slave belonging to Judith Minter, was born on July 1, 1775, and was baptized on July 16, 1775. Kingston Parish Register, p. 82.

William, a slave belonging to Judith Minter, was born on July 1, 1775, and was baptized on July 16, 1775. Kingston Parish Register, p. 83.

William, a slave belonging to Anna Gayle, was born on August 23, 1775, and was baptized on August 27, 1775. Kingston Parish Register, p. 83.

William, a slave belonging to Isaac Smith, was born in September 1775 and was baptized on October 22, 1775. Kingston Parish Register, p. 83.

William, a slave belonging to Armistead Plummer, was born in July 1776 and was baptized on July 28, 1776. Kingston Parish Register, p. 85.

William, a slave belonging to George Brooks, was born in September or October 1776 and was baptized on December 1, 1776. Kingston Parish Register, p. 86.

William Howe, a slave belonging to Walter Keeble, was baptized on January 4, 1779. Kingston Parish Register, p. 89.

Wilson, Ben. See Ben Wilson.

Winny or Wenner, a slave belonging to Capt. George Dudley, was baptized on April 16, 1750. Kingston Parish Register, p. 83.

Winny or Whenny, a slave belonging to Joseph Digges, was born in March 1761. Kingston Parish Register, p. 54.

Wonna or Woonah, a slave belonging to Henry Whiting, was born on November 9, 1765. Kingston Parish Register, p. 61.

Woona or Woonah, a slave belonging to John Hayes, was born in June 1769. Kingston Parish Register, p. 65.

Woona, a slave belonging to George Dudley, was born in February 1776 and was baptized on April 28, 1776. Kingston Parish Register, p. 84.

Woona, a slave belonging to George William Plummer, was born in March 1776 and was baptized on June 16, 1776. Kingston Parish Register, p. 85.

Y

York, a slave belonging to Isaac Jones, was born in July 1772 and was baptized on August 23, 1772. Kingston Parish Register, p. 71.

Slaveholders Listed in the Parish Register and Years of Reporting

Adams (Addams),
Christopher 1773–1775
Almon,
    Joel 1772
Anderson,
    Edward 1764–1775
Armistead,
    Ann 1750–1758
    Anna 1752–1759
    Currel 1768–1773
    Dorothy 1776
    Francis 1767–1773
    Francis's estate 1775
    George 1771–1777
    John 1750–1774
    John's estate 1774–1777
    Ralph 1759
    Robert 1775–1777
    William 1750–1775
    Mr. 1750
    Mrs. 1750
Barnet (Barnett),
    Peter 1774
Bentley,
    Sally 1774
    William 1769
Bernard (Barnard),
    Peter 1772–1777
    Robert 1754–1760
    William 1772–1773
Billups,
    Anna 1771–1777
    Elizabeth 1756–1765
    Humphrey 1757–1772
    John Sr. 1750–1769
    John 1753–1777
John Jr. 1763–1766
John (Captain) 1772–1775
    Joseph 1757–1773
    Langley 1750–1771
    Langley's estate 1771–1772
    Langley's widow 1773
    Nancy 1777
    Richard 1750

    Robert 1756–1777
    Robert (Captain) 1767–1775
    Thomas 1773–1777
Blacknall (Blacknal),
    Ann 1755
    Charles 1750–1761
    Mary 1765–1776
    Mr. 1750
Blake,
    Thomas 1774
Bohannon (Bohannan, Bohonnan),
    William 1777
Bond,
    William 1753–1758
Borum (Boram),
    Edmund 1751–1777
    Edmund Sr. 1775–1776
    Mr. 1774
Boswell,
    Thomas (Captain) 1766–1771
    Bristow (Bristoe),
    Robert (Major) 1754
Bristow Estate [no first name]
1756–1771
    Robert's estate 1767–1777
Brooks (Brookes),
    Ann 1757–1768
    Dorothy 1762
    George 1771–1776
    Richard 1770–1773
    Thomas 1750–1763
    Mr. 1750
    Mr.'s estate 1750
Brown,
    Christopher 1770–1774
    George 1757–1774
    Richard 1758
Buckner,
    William 1775–1777
Burton,
    Ann 1777
    Charles 1777
Callis (Calles, Callice, Callise,
Callys),
    James 1747–1758

James Sr. 1752
James Jr. 1758
John 1757
William 1756–1771
Carter,
    James 1777
    Jane 1774–1777
    John 1774
Cary (Carey),
    Alexander 1760–1762
    Ann 1774
    Dorothy 1772–1777
    James 1772
    John 1750
    John Jr. 1750–1768
    John Sr. 1753–1767
    John's estate 1769
    Mary 1773
    Widow 1750
    Widow (North River) 1777
Clayton,
    Jasper 1771–1777
    John (Capt.) 1771
    John 1771
Cook (Cooke),
    Mordecai 1756–1758
Cully (Culley),
    Christopher 1768–1776
    Robert 1768–1776
Cunningham (Cuningham),
    Mrs. Mary 1746–1748
    Mary 1760
    Mrs. 1750
Curtis,
    Augustine 1771–1774
    Edmund 1768–1775
Davis,
    Edward 1755–1781
    Humphrey
    (Humphry) 1768–1776
    Isaac 1762–1777
    James 1757–1777
    John 1754–1767
    John Sr. 1759–1761
    John (sheriff) 1759–1761
    Joseph 1751–1775
    Joyce 1772–1774
    Mrs. Mary 1772

Susanna 1756
Thomas 1773–1776
Dawson,
    Christopher 1768–1770
    Mr. 1750
Debman (Debnam),
    Charles 1775–1776
    Mr. 1750
Digges (Degge, Degges, Diggs),
    Anthony 1753–1764
    Anthony Jr. 1754
    Augustine 1773
    [no first name] 1773
    Francis 1758–1765
    John 1776
    Joseph 1761–1777
    Mary 1775–1777
Dixon (Dickson),
    John (Rev.) 1753–1777
    John (Capt.) 1777
    Tinsley (Tindsley) 1770–1776
Dudley,
    Dorothy (widow) 1777
    George (Capt.) 1750
    George 1764–1776
    George Sr. 1774
    George Alexander 1769–1777
    Major 1750
    Mrs. Mary 1759
Dunbar,
    Mary 1757–1763
Eddins (Eddens, Edden),
    Dawson 1769–1775
    John 1752–1776
    John Jr. 1772
    John Sr. 1775
    Samuel 1774–1776
Eldris,
    Mr. 1750
Elliott (Elliot),
    John 1772–1777
    John Jr. 1771
    John Sr. 1775
    William 1750, 1773–1776
Fitchett (Fitchet),
    Daniel 1769–1773
Fitzhugh,
    George 1776
    Mr. 1777

Flippin (Flippen, Flipping),
    John 1772
    Robert 1752
Forrest,
    George 1761–1774
    Harry 1750
    Henry 1770–1776
    Sarah 1750–1766
    Thomas 1752–1756
Foster,
    Isaac 1775
    James 1772
    Joel 1766–1777
    John 1753–1777
    John Jr. 1769–1773
    John Sr. 1769–1775
    Joshua 1771–1774
    Josiah 1762–1776
    Richard 1769
    Robert 1765–1769
Gayle (Gale),
    Anna 1775
    Christopher 1760–1771
    Christopher's estate
    1772–1773
    John 1757–1774
    Joseph 1756–1766
    Joshua 1769–1774
    Josiah 1754–1776
    Joyce 1774
    Matthew (Mathew) 1776
    Robert 1776–1777
    Sarah 1774
    Thomas 1766
    Widow 1772
Green,
    Elizabeth 1756–1763
    Robert 1776–1777
Gwyn (Gwynn, Guine, Guin),
    Harry 1752–1777
    Hwney 1771–1776
    Hugh 1750–1775
    Humphrey
    (Humphry) 1770–1776
    John 1750–1767
    John (son of H. G.) 1772
    Lucy 1771
    Richard 1763–1768
    William 1750–1761
    Mrs. 1750
    Widow 1750

Hackney,
    Jacob 1775
Harper,
    Banister (Bannister) 1772
    James 1760–1776
Harris,
    James 1773–1775
    Josiah 1773
Hayes,
    James 1750–1753
    John 1750–1777
    Mary 1765–1776
    Thomas 1758–1777
    Thomas Jr. 1753–1768
    Thomas (Capt.) 1752–1773
    William 1750–1768
    William (Capt.) 1762–1771
    William (Capt.'s) estate 1771
Hewel (Hewil, Huel, Huell),
    John 1760–1767
    Thomas 1772–1775
Hodges,
    Ann 1774
    Benjamin 1750
    James 1757
    William 1750
Holder,
    Elizabeth 1758–1775
Hudgins (Hudgens, Hudgen),
    Edward 1773
    Holder (Houlder) 1775
    Hugh 1772–1776
    Humphrey
    (Humphry) 1771–1776
    John 1770–1776
    Lukey 1775
    Mary 1773
    Moses 1756–1760
    Thomas 1776
    William 1761–1777
    Widow 1774
Hughes,
    Edward 1758–1776
    Gabriel 1764–1777
Humphrey (Humphry),
    Richard 1750
Hunley (Hundley),
    Ann 1756–1759
    Caleb 1755

Esther 1764–1767
George 1757–1769
Henry 1777
James 1772–1776
James (carpenter) 1774
John 1762
John's estate 1768
Richard 1750
Robert 1757–1777
Sarah 1764
Wilkinson 1757–1763
William 1753–1774
Widow 1772

Hurst,
John 1767–1775
Richard 1774
William 1773

Iverson (Iveson),
Susannah 1763
Thomas 1775–1776
Thomas's estate 1770–1777
Widow 1772

James,
Matthias 1755–1776
Thomas 1795–1826

Jarvis (Jervis, Jarvice),
Banister 1752
Betty 1776
John 1750
Lindsey 1772
William 1776

Jones,
Charles 1752–1773
Charles' estate 1775
Elizabeth 1774–1777
Isaac 1772
James 1754
Philip Edward 1777
Thomas 1772
Widow 1750–1777

Keeble (Keebler),
George 1750–1754
Walter 1758–1779
Mr. 1750

Keys (Keyes, Kees),
John 1757–1771

Kemp,
William 1774–1775
Kerr (Car, Carr),
Andrew 1772–1777
King,
John 1773–1776
Joseph 1773–1777
Kingston Parish
1749
Knight,
Henry 1776–1777
Lewis,
Eleanor 1750
Elizabeth 1767
John 1768–1777
John's estate 1769
Estate [no first name] 1769
Lucretia 1771
Thomas 1761–1763
Thomas's estate 1770
Lilly (Lilley),
Elizabeth 1761–1765
Frances 1765
John 1756–1764
Mildred 1762
Roseanna (Rose
Anna) 1762–1774
William 1763–1777
Lowry,
Mary 1773–1776
Lux,
Elizabeth 1764–1775
Mrs. 1771–1776
Machen (Michen),
John 1759–1776
Lucy 1764–1768
Margaret 1764–1776
Thomas 1750–1754
Thomas (Capt.) 1756–1757
Thomas's estate 1763
Marchant (Merchant),
Ambrose 1762–1775
Daniel 1775
Richard 1753–1759
Richard's estate 1774–1776
William 1772–1777
Matthews (Mathews),
Ann 1774

Dorothy 1774
Edward 1775
Richard 1773
Robert 1771–1777
Miller (Millar),
    Anderson 1775
    Catherine 1757
    Francis 1771–1773
    Gabriel 1764–1776,
    1799–1803
    Joannah 1759
    James 1775–1776
    Joseph 1772–1774
Minter (Mintor),
    Judith 1772–1775
    William 1769
Morris,
    William's estate 1776
Newell (Newel),
    John 1756–1758
Nuttall,
    John 1767
Page,
    John 1771–1774
    Mann 1774–1775
Palmer,
    Lucy 1769
Parsons,
    James 1774–1777
Peade (Pead, Peed),
    James 1763–1772
Peyton,
    John 1750–1771
    John (Capt.) 1753–1767
    John (Sir) 1770–1777
Plummer,
    Armistead 1776
    George William 1771–1776
    Judith 1773–1775
    Judith (Mrs.) 1773–1774
    Kemp (Capt.) 1750–1758
    Kemp 1759–1764
    Kemp's estate 1771
    Kemp (Major) 1760–1771
    Kemp's (Major) estate 1771
    Mary 1774–1776
    William 1764–1770

William (Capt.) 1757–1766
William (Major) 1767–1774
William's estate 1774
Pool (Poole),
    Thomas 1750–1776
Pritchard,
    Joseph 1760
Purcell,
    James 1763–1774
Ransone (Ranson),
    Ann 1753
    James 1749–1765
    Letitia 1750–1777
    Richard 1770–1771
Read (Reade),
    Benjamin 1768
    Dorothy 1763
    Gwyn 1749–1752
    Gwyn (Capt.) 1750–1754
    Gwyn's estate 1766
    John of Middlesex
    County 1750
    John's estate 1750–1760
    Mildred 1772
    Milly 1774
    Robert 1750–1773
Respess (Respes, Respiss),
    John 1760–1770
    Joyce 1773
    Richard 1772–1775
    Thomas 1773
    William 1772
Ripley,
    John 1763–1773
Robinson,
    John (Major) 1774
    [no first name] 1775
Roots (Rootes),
    John 1761–1766
Samson (Sampson),
    John 1771
Shackleford,
    Benjamin 1775–1776
Singleton,
    Anthony 1761–1763
Smith,
    Isaac 1764–1776

Peter 1771–1776
Robert 1752
Sarah 1769
Thomas 1756–1774
Thomas (Captain) 1760–1774
Thomas (Major) 1774–1777
Madam 1750
Mr. 1750
Spencer (Spenser),
    Catherine 1762–1774
    R. (Mr.) 1770
    Robert 1769–1775
    Widow 1750
Stevens,
    William 1775
Stewart (Stuart),
    William 1771–1774, 1776
Tabb (Tab),
    Edward 1776
    Francis 1772–1774
    Franky 1772
    John 1772–1775
    Susanna 1773–1775
    Toy's estate 1771–1772
    William 1750
    Mrs. 1772
Thomas,
    Ann 1763
    Humphrey (Humphry) 1756
    James 1773–1777
Thornton,
    Sterling 1774
Tompkins (Tomkins),
    Hannah 1776

John 1772–1774
John's estate 1775–1776
Robert 1764–1771
William 1760–1767
Turner,
    Ann 1766
    George 1763
Westcomb (Westcom),
    Nicholas 1774
White (Whitt),
    Mary 1807
    William 1761–1773
Whiting,
    Henry 1765–1770
    John 1771
    Kemp 1759–1761
    Mathew 1762–1771
    Robert (Capt.) 1750–1754
Wiley,
    John 1777
Willis,
    John 1771–1775
Williams,
    Daniel 1755–1775
    Samuel 1775–1777
    Capt. 1765
Window (Winder),
    John 1764
    Rose's estate 1760
Wyatt (Wiatt),
    Margaret 1773–1777
Peter 1756

INDEX